Schools of Sympathy is a feminist exploration of gender and identification in Samuel Richardson's *Clarissa*, Nathaniel Hawthorne's *The Scarlet Letter*, Henry James's *Portrait of a Lady*, and Thomas Hardy's *Tess of the D'Urbervilles*. In each of these novels the heroine is portrayed as a victim. Nancy Roberts examines how the reader's sympathy for the heroines is constructed, the motivations and desires involved in an identification with victimization, and the gender and power roles that such an identification calls into play.

Roberts argues that the "heroism" or "greatness" of each of these heroines is measured not by her actions but by the extent to which others are moved by her. Thus the character cannot be studied without studying the response she generates, which, in these novels, is sympathy. Roberts asserts that each of the novels can be understood as a school of sympathy, through which we learn to behave and feel as gendered subjects, and that our response to the heroine is as carefully crafted as the character herself.

Schools of Sympathy addresses the issues of masochism, female victimization, the power of passive seduction, and the possibilities of heroism. As a counterpoint to these eighteenth- and nineteenth-century male perspectives, Roberts examines works by Margaret Atwood and Angela Carter that explicitly address these issues.

NANCY ROBERTS is an instructor of English, Langara College.

Schools of Sympathy

Gender and Identification through the Novel

NANCY ROBERTS

The University of British Columbia
Academic Women's Association

McGill-Queen's University Press
Montreal & Kingston · London · Buffalo

This book is dedicated to Vinit, Arjun, and Gita

© McGill-Queen's University Press 1997
ISBN 0-7735-1668-9 (cloth)
ISBN 0-7735-1685-9 (paper)

Legal deposit fourth quarter 1997
Bibliothèque nationale du Québec

Printed in Canada on acid-free paper

This book has been published with the help of a grant from the Humanities and Social Sciences Federation of Canada, using funds provided by the Social Sciences and Humanities Research Council of Canada.

McGill-Queen's University Press acknowledges the support received for its publishing program from the Canada Council's Block Grants program.

Canadian Cataloguing in Publication Data

Roberts, Nancy, 1948-
    Schools of sympathy: gender and identification through the novel
Co-published by the University of British Columbia, Academic
    Women's Association.
Includes bibliographical references and index.
ISBN 0-7735-1668-9 (bound)
ISBN 0-7735-1685-9 (pbk.)
1. English fiction—History and criticism.   2. Women in literature.
3. Sex role in literature.   4. Gender identity in literature.   I. UBC
Academic Women's Association.   II. Title.
PR830.H4R62 1997   820.9'352042   C97-900559-0

Published in co-operation with the University of British Columbia
Academic Women's Association

Consulting Editor
Dianne Newell

Editorial Board, UBC Academic Women's Association:
Dianne Newell, Department of History and Faculty of Graduate
    Studies and General Editor
Alison Buchan, Department of Physiology
Diana Lary, Department of History

Contents

Foreword

Nancy Roberts' study of the role that reading novels can play in the formation of gender positioning, *Schools of Sympathy: Gender and Identification in Novels*, is included in the Academic Women's Association series because of its original contribution to the field of gender studies. Roberts argues that the process of reading novels helps form gender positioning. The novels function as "schools of sympathy" which teach us, in her words, "to act and feel as gendered subjects" (p. 10). The work is based on Roberts' doctoral research in the Department of English at the University of British Columbia, for which she won the Academic Women's Association's A. Jean Elder prize for the outstanding dissertation in the arts and social sciences completed in 1993.

The Academic Women's Association at the University of British Columbia promotes exciting new fields of women's scholarly inquiry by encouraging the publication of research results. *Schools of Sympathy* is the third in the AWA's book series.

The first volume in the series is a work of history by Lee Stewart, *"It's Up To You": Women at UBC in the Early Years* (Vancouver: UBC Press 1990). Based on Stewart's graduate research at UBC, it was intended as the AWA's contribution to the university's seventy-fifth anniversary celebrations. Stewart examines the experience and strategies of female advocates, educators, and students against the background of the social and cultural conditions prior to the revolutionary decade of the 1960s.

The second volume, *Women, Work, and Coping: A Multidisciplinary Approach to Workplace Stress* (Montreal and Kingston: McGill-Queen's University Press, 1993), edited by Bonita Long and Sharon Kahn, takes as its focus employed women and investigates the special issue of coping with workplace stress today. It is a collection of original scholarly essays by North American scholars commissioned by Long and Kahn; both are professors in the Department of Counselling Psychology, Faculty of Education, University of British Columbia, who have been researching and writing on the subject since the early 1980s. The contribution by Allison Tom, "Women's Lives Complete: Methodological Concerns," received the Canadian Research Institute for the Advancement of Women's annual Marion Porter Prize for the most significant feminist research article.

McGill-Queen's University Press will publish a fourth volume in the series in 1997: Laura Cameron's *Openings: A Mediation on History, Method, and Sumas Lake. Openings* is a work of interdisciplinary historical scholarship. The research was undertaken for her graduate programme in history at the University of British Columbia. She is completing her doctorate in historical geography at Cambridge University.

On behalf of the AWA I wish to thank my colleagues on the editorial board, Alison Buchan and Diana Lary, and the current AWA Chair, Susan Kennedy, Director of the Occupational Hygiene Programme, Faculty of Graduate Studies. Philip Cercone, director and executive editor of McGill-Queen's University Press, has once again offered much-needed support at a critical stage of the project. A special thanks to the press staff, especially Aurèle Parisien and Joan McGilvray. This manuscript won a much-appeciated grant-in-aid of publication from the Social Science Federation of Canada, using funds provided by the Social Sciences and Humanities Research Council of Canada. Finally, I wish to acknowledge the backing of the president of UBC, David Strangway, and the vice-president and provost, Daniel R. Birch. Several years ago Dr Strangway authorized a generous grant from the University Development Fund to support the AWA book series and more recently authorized additional funding to help with the special production needs of this book.

Dianne Newell
General Editor
AWA series

Preface

The story of this book may not be quite so arresting or moving as the story of Clarissa Harlowe or Tess Durbeyfield, but I think the outline of its genesis and its obsessions might be instructive nonetheless. This is a story about women and reading. As a lifelong reader of novels, I know how they have shaped and, to some extent, determined the person I've become.

I was lucky that when I returned to graduate school I found it convulsed in "theory." This was a time of great excitement. Most exciting to me were the connections being made – connections between and among literature, history, politics, and philosophy. There was a sense at that time that all we might have taken for granted was now under question. As a feminist I welcomed this shaking of the pillars of convention. From all the tumult and confusion of this time I took what I needed for this project. From Foucault I took a way of conceptualizing the social and historical formation of the subject. From film theorists I began to appreciate the way that narrative and film situate us, "put us in our place" both in the cinema and in society at large. And from feminism, always, was the renewed conviction that the personal is political (an outlook feminism shares with Foucault), a continued questioning of the *status quo*, and a way to approach fiction that could show how much it mattered.

Rereading *Clarissa* and *Tess* in preparation for my Ph.D. candidacy exams, I was struck anew by the prolonged misery of these tales. As I read, I felt myself to be in the grip of a voice or narrative that would not let me be, a voice that demanded that I look and keep on looking at the spectacle it provided, a spectacle of what seemed to be infinite female woe. Things were bad for these heroines and they just got worse. Compelled to read and to suffer along with them, I both resented and, in a perverse kind of way, enjoyed the experience. Although I hated reading these books, I could not stop reading them. What was going on? What accounted for my own reaction, and more important, why did I *have* to read these? Why were these tales of victimization, cruelty, and suffering given such a central place in the canon? It was reactions and questions such as these that provided the genesis of this study.

Since then, this work has taken on a life of its own, bringing me to places, like the world of Angela Carter, that I hadn't known existed. Places that give me hope for the future.

We have recently passed through a period of social history in which the very word "victim" has grown, at least to some, tiresome and troubling. In the era of identity politics victim status has been claimed, denied, debated, ridiculed, and abandoned by one group after another. It is my hope that by looking at these early and contemporary novels we can begin to see what is being contested, to understand why the figure of victim should be at once so compelling and so problematic.

Acknowledgments

I owe a great deal of thanks to the many people who have helped make this book a reality. It was in Peter Buitenhuis' seminar at SFU that I first started reading Hawthorne next to James. At UBC I was fortunate to have Nick Hudson, Eva-Marie Kröller, and Sherrill Grace on my supervisory committee. Their support throughout the lengthy dissertation process was invaluable. In their comments and responses I received both challenge and encouragement. But I want to single out Sherrill Grace in particular for her care and enthusiasm in helping me with this project. I feel very lucky to have had her as a supervisor. Her warmth, generosity, and tenacity helped pull me through.

My second round of thanks is to The Academic Women's Association at UBC, who have honored me with both their annual award and the inclusion of this book in their publishing series. Dianne Newell has been an extraordinary "fairy godmother" in this respect, encouraging, cajoling, and offering many hours of help and suppport.

I have been fortunate in my editors at McGill-Queens as well. Aurèle Parisien, Joan McGilvray, and Frances Rooney have helped me throughout. Their close attention, good questions, and enthusiasm have been very much needed and appreciated. Ann Mckinnon was a great help in pulling together an index.

I also want to acknowledge the support of my colleagues at Langara College. Their warmth, good sense, and great humour have kept me going and made my task much easier. The students in my fall 1996 women's studies class are also to be thanked. We explored *Nights at the Circus* together, and their enthusiasm and insights inspired me to look again at a novel I thought I already knew.

Finally, I turn to my mother, Barbara Roberts, my husband, Vinit Khosla, and my children, Arjun and Gita. Without their unfailing encouragement, patience and love, none of this would have been possible.

Schools of Sympathy

1 Schools of Sympathy

"It is my design to make thee feel."[1] With these words John Belford, Clarissa Harlowe's friend and protector, announces his intention to Lovelace, who is himself both Belford's best friend and Clarissa's tormentor. The design that Belford claims as his own is actually the intention of the novel as well. It is *Clarissa*'s design to make us feel. The plight of its heroine is presented in order to arouse an emotional response. Her suffering becomes our own (tortured) pleasure. With this epigraph, I chart out the territory of my own project. It is my design both to show how novels (*Clarissa* and others) teach us to feel and to explore the way that these structures of feeling serve to produce, replicate, and impose positions of power and gender.

If I am to rely on Belford's words to this extent, I want to pay attention to the exact terms of his address. There are several points to note. The first is the very deliberation and force in Belford's "design": Lovelace has to be *made* to feel. It seems that one cannot rely on a spontaneous eruption of the right sort of feeling; its construction must instead be designed and then applied. Nothing is to be taken for granted, so the good reader and the good emotional response must be produced by the text. This is true for all the novels considered in this study.[2]

The second point to note is that the transaction, as presented in

Belford's statement, is exclusively male. The primary focus of the novel – Clarissa and her plight – shifts in this passage onto the relationship between Lovelace and Belford. One man writes to another in order to make him "feel." The arousal of emotion is the goal.[3] Such an arousal provides pleasure, for in this instance Belford is *gratified* to learn that Lovelace is angry at him. "It gives me pleasure," he writes, "to find my intention answered" (4:367). This evocation of emotion is at once moral, sadistic, and intimate. It is moral in that Belford wants Lovelace to feel the effects of what he has done to Clarissa, wants him to experience remorse. It is sadistic because Belford does not care if – may even prefer that – the experience of remorse causes Lovelace pain. Finally, the statement is intimate because it gives Belford pleasure to excite Lovelace. This is an intimacy that is neither kind nor comfortable, but which allows one man access to the emotional life of the other.

The third point is the logical corollary of the second. To speak of this as a male transaction is to acknowledge its elision of the figure of Clarissa. She exists here only to the extent that she moves others to feel. In other words, her suffering, or more accurately, the representation of that suffering (as it is reported to Lovelace, or as it is reported to us) is of less importance than its effects. It comes to function as a token or item of exchange between men. Since Clarissa and her suffering have worth only to the extent that they produce feeling, her pain and her own feelings become commodified counters in an economy of emotion. This was, of course, Eve Kosofsky Sedgwick's argument in *Between Men*. Her point, derived in part from the work of Claude Lévi-Strauss and Gayle Rubin, was that "patriarchal heterosexuality can best be discussed in terms of one or another form of traffic in women: it is the use of women as exchangeable, perhaps symbolic, property for the primary purpose of cementing the bonds of men with men."[4] The bond between Lovelace and Belford is strengthened through their appreciation of Clarissa's pain.

There is one final point to be made about this paradigmatic exchange between Lovelace and Belford, a point which, while considerably complicating the last, does not, as it may appear, contradict it. While it is true that Clarissa's actual suffering is less important than its effects on both characters and readers, the creation of those effects, our feelings, *depends* on her and her pain. Belford and Lovelace may be locked in a moral, sadistic, and intimate exchange that only *uses* Clarissa, but they need her. They get to each other *through* her. Their feelings for her enable them to feel (for) each other. She is the agent that produces feeling, and this gives her power.

Let me reiterate the four ideas which this epigraph suggests, points which I will be exploring throughout this study. These are: that the emotional effect of a novel is both plotted and enforced; that the emotional exchange (between Lovelace and Belford in the example, or between author and reader in the novels explored here) appears to be – at least paradigmatically – structured as an inherently male activity; that the female protagonist in such a transaction becomes reduced to a mere counter or token of exchange between men; and finally, whether in spite of this reduction, or because of it, the heroine gains a type of power from her position.

HEROINE AS VICTIM

The status of the novels considered in the central section of this study, *Clarissa, The Scarlet Letter, The Portrait of a Lady*, and *Tess of the d'Urbervilles*, bears testimony to this negative power. Long considered to be among the greatest novels in English literature, their place in the canon has been pre-eminent and secure. The heroines of these novels have enjoyed similar prestige. Clarissa Harlowe, Hester Prynne, Isabel Archer, and Tess Durbeyfield have assumed exemplary status in our culture. Because their stories have been read and taught for decades in the schools and universities of Britain, North America, and the rest of the world, they have come to enjoy a sort of emblematic status. But of what are these heroines emblems; what do they represent? As icons of womanhood in Western culture, what do they tell us about our culture and the place of woman within it?

Each of these heroines is represented as, to some extent, choosing her own victimization. Clarissa is but half tricked out of her father's house, and spends her last days making her death and funeral into elaborate works of art. Hester voluntarily returns to Massachusetts and takes up her scarlet letter again "of her own free will" long after there is any need to be punished. Isabel also apparently returns to her miserable marriage, rejecting all offers of love or escape. Tess is portrayed as one of a long line of passive victims, helpless against her fate. In the end she lies on an altar at Stonehenge and waits for the police to take her away. The novels tell us there is heroism in these sacrifices. They tell us that it is in the heroines' embrace of tragedy that their greatness lies, that self-sacrifice and self-destruction represent woman's highest calling and her deepest desire. Furthermore, these novels teach us that such acts are particularly thrilling when they are observed and approved by others, that being a victim brings attention.

In the figure of the heroine/victim is conjoined the activity of the hero and the passivity of the victim. Such a conjunction raises perplexing problems. One of these is that the "heroism" or "greatness" of the heroine is measured by means other than her actions. For she can *do*, can *move*, very little. (After all, as victim she is less an actor than one who is acted upon.) Her heroism is measured instead by the pity and sympathy she elicits from others, by the extent to which she *moves* them (us). What this means for reading is that we cannot study the character herself without studying the response she generates. A study of character becomes a study of response, a study of both the responses represented *in* the text (that is, by the other characters to the heroine) and of our *own* responses as readers.[5]

It can be argued, for example, that Clarissa is empty except as a figure established to elicit the admiration and sympathy of others. Similarly, Hester Prynne is defined by the letter A which draws and shapes our attention. Isabel Archer is, in one sense, only a magnet for a group of people who seek to live through her. Ralph Touchett, Caspar Goodwood, and Lord Warburton gather around her, touched and saddened by her fate. Tess is an eroticized object whose appeal lies in her passive victimization. In each novel the heroine is placed as an icon, the purpose of which is to draw and invite our response. Often she is represented as having little life or character of her own; her existence is predicated upon our response to her.

Critics, puzzling over this passivity, have sought its source in the heroine herself. They have looked to her "nature," her "character," or her "psyche" in search of clues to her victimization. This type of analysis has prompted some critics to identify and to probe the so-called "dark side" of the heroine, to find out why she has come to such a pass, leading one to claim that "suffering is fatally desirable to Isabel" (McMaster 50) and another to find "substantial insights into Tess's character that help us understand the roots of her self-destructiveness."[6] Some even go as far as V.S. Pritchett, who in 1947 wrote that "Clarissa represents that extreme of puritanism which desires to be raped. Like Lovelace's, her sexuality is really violent, insatiable in its wish for destruction."[7]

We note the repetition of two words in all of these statements. The first is "desire" (suffering is *desirable* for Isabel, Clarissa *desires* to be raped), and the second is "destruction" (Tess is *self-destructive*, Clarissa's sexuality is a wish [desire] for *destruction*). The message is clear: these heroines have sought out their own destruction. It is as if, however reluctantly, the critics have been forced to conclude that our heroines exhibit masochistic tendencies, that each in her own way, "asks for it."[8] Such conclusions resonate for us now at the end of the twentieth century, when in society at large and courts of law in particular, we continue to struggle with issues of woman's "will" and "assent," with issues of power and sex. It is in part this contemporary relevance that makes it so imperative that we look again at these earlier texts to see how both they and their heroines have been read and judged.

THE HEROINE AND HER READERS

The words "desire" and "destruction" appear to be inescapably paired in the critics' assessment of these heroines. But whose desire is it anyway? And whose destruction? How can it be claimed that the heroines are enacting their own desires, when, after all, they have none, when they are merely creations of ink on paper? I prefer to view the novel as a vehicle which constructs and presents such a desire for the readers, granting us a privileged position from which we may both enjoy the representation of the heroine's desire from a distance *and* participate in it through our identification with her. Through this process her desire becomes, at least to some extent, our desire, and if that desire is masochistic, well then so is ours.

As should be clear by now, the nature of this study demands a double focus. Like the critics mentioned above, I will be looking at the heroine herself. But rather than look for clues to her victimization in her nature or her psychology, I will look instead to her representation and its deployment. This means that I focus on those she affects as much as on the heroine herself. I am just as interested in the readers and the sympathy we bear for the heroine as I am in the character. I will be asking whether this sympathy, usually understood as a compassionate and noble emotion, is purely benevolent, or whether its puported charity might conceal motives more troubling and more complex.

Each of the heroines functions as a kind of magnetic void in her novel, a figure passive and empty in herself, but large and active in her effects. As she lies captive, we readers are stirred on her behalf. As she is objectified, we are roused to full subjectivity. Current theory on subjectivity and identification provides a new lens with which to examine these old texts. I will see the extent to which such recent terminology is applicable or even useful in reading these earlier texts. It may be that in this cluster of novels – one eighteenth-century and three nineteenth – we can trace an emerging set of codes and conventions defining the subject and its relations with others. I would like to see to what extent these emerging codes can be related to what we now call identification.

The novels considered in this study span more than two hundred years. The term identification, however, is much more recent. I am going to have to rely on other terms as well, terms like sympathy, empathy, and pity, to trace the nature of the emotional response constructed for the reader over those two hundred years. I will try to show that, although the terms may shift, certain issues of connection, power, and emotion remain intact.

But it is the old-fashioned term "sympathy" that I resurrect for my title. There are several reasons for my choice. In its broadest definition, sympathy, according to the *Random House Dictionary* (2nd ed.), simply means "harmony of or agreement in feeling" (agreement in *any* feeling), but the dictionary goes on to define sympathy further as "sharing the feelings of another, esp. in sorrow or trouble." The addition of "sorrow or trouble" is important. From the shorter unabridged OED we learn that sympathy is derived from the the Greek (pathos), suffering. It is this sense which is dropped from the more modern, psychoanalytic term "identification."

According to Laplanche and Pontalis, identification is "the psychological process whereby *the subject* assimilates an aspect, property or attribute of the other and *is transformed*, wholly or partially, after the model the other provides. It is by means of a series of identifications that the personality is constituted and specified" (205). According to this definition, identification differs from sympathy in that the subject uses the other as a model through which it constructs its personality. This relationship seems to be at least potentially closer, more intimate, than the relationship between sympathizer and victim. Furthermore, identification, as we understand it today, is (at least on the surface) power neutral. The one we identify with may occupy any position, including one equal to ours. The sympathetic relation, by contrast, is not so egalitarian; its connections are more uneasy. As David Marshall points out in *Surprising Effects*, "our sympathy – and the pleasure we seem to take in it – depend on the violence and suffering inflicted on those who appear as spectacles before us"(48). Their pain becomes our aesthetic pleasure.

At the very least, sympathy seems to involve a disquieting combination of distress on behalf of the other along with a sense of self-satisfaction based on our own good fortune and on our capacity to feel. Such self-congratulation may, however, be further complicated by other emotions. Leo Bersani has written that "there is a certain risk in all sympathetic projections ... a secret attachment to scenes of suffering and violence" ("Representation" 150). If this is so, then sympathy is less simple and less benign than is usually supposed. I want to investigate this "secret attachment," find out what it is made of and why it has been so secret. I have already mentioned that critics have "accused" the novels' heroines of masochism. What is our relationship to them? If our pleasure depends upon the heroine's pain, is that pleasure then masochistic as well, or is it sadistic? Does either of these terms apply? To what extent are such terms or categories relevant to our experience? I will be returning to a fuller treatment of these subjects later in the chapter, but my point here is simply that we cannot look at heroine or reader in isolation; our roles and our desires are complex, intertwined and mutually interdependent.

I also choose "sympathy" because of its centrality in at least two of the novels under consideration. Both *Clarissa* and *The Scarlet Letter* focus on the attractions and the dangers of sympathy. *Clarissa* can be read as an extended study on sympathy and its effects. Hawthorne's novel evokes and then subverts earlier eighteenth-century notions of sympathy, playing them off against nineteenth-century romantic assumptions. But all the works studied here explore the emotional connections we have variously labelled sympathy, pity, empathy, or identification. I will be studying each novel's use of these terms and the varying gender and power relations they inscribe.

Recent work in post-structuralist literary theory, particularly in feminist and film studies, has used the work of Foucault, Lacan, and others to challenge and investigate our assumptions about subjectivity and gender.[9] Both Foucault and Lacan have taught us to look at the means by which subjects are created and sexualities are produced and regulated. Foucault has written that "the goal of my work during the last twenty years ... has been to create a history of the diferent modes by which, in our culture, human beings are made subjects" (*Reader* 7). The novel is surely one of these modes. It has been instrumental in creating our sense of ourselves as subjects, and one of its projects seems to be instruction in feeling in general, and sympathy in particular.

Each of the novels under consideration in this study acts as a sort of school of sympathy, a place in which emotions are coached and disciplined, marshalled and pointed in the right direction. Readers see sympathy displayed through the performance of certain key characters who show us how we, in turn, might perform it. Reading is the performance through which we get a chance to rehearse such feelings, try different roles, play out various emotional responses. The novels, then, as sites of instruction, come to serve as social agents doing social work, and our lessons in becoming good subjects necessarily involve lessons in how to act and feel as gendered subjects.

CHOICES

While I would argue that probably all novels can serve as instructional sites or schools of feeling, I would not say that all have the same lessons to teach. Nor would I claim that the novels and the heroines studied here are representative of some grand category such as "Eighteenth- and Nineteenth-Century Literature" or "Female Characters in Fiction." To do so would be to ignore those strong, determined, and more successful heroines such as Elizabeth Bennett, Jane Eyre, Dorothea Brooke, or Becky Sharpe. I chose these particular texts because of the similarities in their heroines' positons and fates; strong, passionate, and virtuous, each is nevertheless in some sense trapped.

One factor determining my choice was that the heroine's suffering be central and emblematic, thereby focalizing certain problems in reader identification. The suffering each heroine undergoes is presented as to some degree instructive or ennobling. There is a lesson for us in her pain. I am interested in seeing what that lesson should be. By choosing novels in which *one* figure takes on the central role of sufferer, and in which that character is female (as opposed to *Middlemarch* or *Caleb Williams*, for example) the routes of identification and sympathy, complicated enough at the best of times, are simplified to the extent that coherent study is made possible.

The second reason is my interest in the cross-gender identification explored in these novels. Each of these books acts as a sort of school of sympathy, a site of instruction in feeling and subjectivity, and the lessons which are offered are, for the most part, gender encoded. Much of what we are taught to feel for Clarissa or for Isabel Archer comes via a central male character, a Belford or a Ralph Touchett, a man who feels her situation acutely, who *appreciates* her pain. Through such male characters we readers learn to feel *for*, and perhaps *as*, a woman. I will be examining this cross-gender mediation, the way that all readers can only reach the heroine through the sympathetic responses of her male admirers. I will be asking what it is about the plight of the heroine/victim that invites both sympathy (sorrow for her troubles) *and* identification (a desire to *be* her, to experience her pain *and* her power). I hope that by focusing on these four canonical texts of the eighteenth and nineteenth centuries alongside four fictional works from the twentieth century, I can isolate and examine certain key features in the reader's response to suffering female characters.

This study falls into two parts. The first deals with the four canonical texts mentioned above. The second section jumps to the twentieth century. Here I turn to two contemporary feminist writers to see how they "talk back" to a tradition that has, in many cases, defined them and their heroines as "other" or as passive and helpless victims. Margaret Atwood and Angela Carter are two highly conscious and articulate writers who directly address the issues raised in the first five chapters: victimization, masochism, the powers of passive seduction, and the possibilities of heroism. Both use their fiction to look simultaneously to the future *and* to the past. Their self-conscious retrospection, coupled with their equally strong interest in the future, drew me to these texts. It is my hope that by holding these books up to the earlier ones, we can see something of both where we have been and where we might be going.

Atwood's *Surfacing* is about constructing an identity in response to perceived victimization. *The Handmaid's Tale*, on the other hand, while appearing to address the politics of oppression, seems to me to merely sensationalize and even eroticize that state. I will question whether Atwood's savvy and stinging analysis ultimately offers us any hope, any way out. Does the novel offer the reader an identification significantly different from that provided by the earlier texts? Angela Carter's work, on the other hand, is offered as a more successful attempt to understand an old dilemma and to imagine some new solutions. *The Bloody Chamber*, Carter's reworking of fairy tales takes us back to some of the earliest narratives of female heroism and female entrapment. In reworking these tales, in imagining them anew, Carter presents the old fears and the old dangers while still offering new possibilities of escape or triumph. In *Nights at the Circus* the reader glimpses a world of female heroism and possibility that is exciting, dangerous – and never simple. Such a view, and such a world, reroute and reconnect the worn-out paths of our desires and our identifications.

The pairing of four classical and canonical texts with four contemporary works may be unorthodox, but it is through such pairings and such couplings that new light is shed on old assumptions. It is in the light of *Clarissa*, *The Scarlet Letter*, *The Portrait of a Lady*, and *Tess* that we can better appreciate what Atwood and Carter are attempting, can better judge the extent of their success.

Most of the works examined here accomplish their lessons in sympathy through the use of a central female character, a heroine whom I have described as empty. Drawing on recent feminist theory on subjectivity and desire, I will consider the significance of these representations of female suffering, investigating how femininity, passivity, and masochism have been linked. Central to my argument is the idea that this figure is no exception or aberration, but is instead representative of a larger socio/political dynamic in which women's power has been feared, controlled and prohibited. The philosophical roots of this situation will be explored in the next section.

"THE IMPOSSIBLE PLACE OF FEMALE DESIRE"

Teresa de Lauretis has written of "the (impossible) place of a purely *passive* desire"(*Alice* 69, 151). The phrase is particularly apt for my purpose since I will be arguing that it just such a desire which is created for both heroines and readers in *Clarissa*, *Scarlet Letter*, *Portrait of a Lady* and *Tess* and which Atwood and Carter's heroines seek to escape. Since desire is most commonly understood as a state which precedes activity or action, a passive desire could only be a contradiction in terms, an *impossibility*. And yet, Lauretis and others would argue that it is out of just such a place that woman's subjectivity has been constructed.

Critics, drawn to what they call the "dark side" of Tess, Isabel, Clarissa, and Hester, have seen it as a self-destructive or masochistic tendency, but I argue that such an apparent masochism is merely an enactment of the paradox of a passive desire. When we turn to the work of Carter and Atwood, we will be looking to see whether their heroines continue to enact this paradox.

In order to consider the twin "problems" of female desire and female subjectivity and trace the ways these have been linked to masochism, I start with a question asked by the feminist psychologist and theorist, Jessica Benjamin: "How does it come about that femininity appears inextricably linked to passivity, even to masochism, or that women seek their desire in another, hope to have it recognized and recognizable through the subjectivity of another?" ("Desire 85). Benjamin's question is central. Where does this desire for self-sacrifice and self-destruction come from, and why/how has it been so insistently linked to femininity?

Many theorists, in attempting to explain this situation, have returned to Simone de Beauvoir's contention in *The Second Sex* that woman can only be thought of as the "Other," can only be described or known in relation to "man" which constitutes the norm.[10] Woman, in this view, serves as spectacle to attract the active and controlling male gaze. She is the heroine over whom men fight, the exchanged commodity in a masculine economy, but she herself can find no active role to play. Her image is everywhere (in Western art as madonna or the nude), but she seems to have no voice, no gaze of her own. When her story is told, it becomes, in Teresa de Lauretis' words, "like any other story, a question of his desire" (*Alice*, 133). It is her presence as mute spectacle, however, that enables the construction of active gaze and full voice in others. She becomes the nothing out of which meaning is made. As Mary Jacobus puts it, "In this theoretical scheme [French feminism], femininity itself – heterogeneity, Otherness – becomes the repressed term by which discourse is made possible" (*Women Writing* 12).

Belford and Lovelace use Clarissa and her suffering to forge their own correspondence and intimacy. Out of her annihilation an entire novel is constructed.

When Jacobus refers to the theoretical scheme of French feminism, she is gesturing toward the work of, among others, Luce Irigaray. In *This Sex which is not One*, Irigaray claims that sexuality and desire have been defined and constructed in Western culture in such a way as to have become exclusively masculine: "Female sexuality," she claims, "has always been conceptualized on the basis of masculine parameters" (23). If this is so, then it becomes almost impossible to imagine what female desire would be since, according to Irigaray, it has been so ruthlessly repressed. She imagines it as something to "be recovered only in secret, in hiding, with anxiety and guilt" (30). Repressed to such an extent, it can only be described by what it is *not*: "Woman's desire would not be expected to speak the same language as man's; woman's desire has doubtless been submerged by the logic that has dominated the West since the time of the Greeks" (25).

Irigaray seems to be saying that there is, or might once have been, an essential female desire which has since been lost or repressed. Having lost her own desire in the service of the patriarchy, Irigaray wonders how woman can participate in what seems to be an absolutely masculine economy: "Woman, in this sexual imaginary, is only a more or less obliging prop for the enactment of man's fantasies. That she may find pleasure there in that role, by proxy, is possible, even certain. But such pleasure is above all a masochistic prostitution of her body to a desire that is not her own" (25).

Woman participates, then, in masculine desire, and may even derive pleasure from it, but for Irigaray such pleasure is always at – at least – one remove. By identifying with and feeling through her lover, her pleasure becomes vicarious and even masochistic. She feels by "proxy," becomes a type of masochist by converting what, Irigaray would say, must be her own disinterest and displeasure into an alienated kind of pleasure by identifying with the desire of her lover. Such an identification, Irigaray insists, creates "a desire that is not her own," and makes it difficult if not impossible to discover what her own might be.

Recalling Woolf's statement that a woman needs a room of her own, Irigaray's own call for woman to seek a desire of her own has become a familiar feminist move. A system is recognized as masculine in nature, as alien to the feminine, and is thereby rejected. Woman is urged to assert her difference, to name her identity as *not*-man. In this case it is the structure and economy of desire itself that is masculine, that represents "a desire that is not her own."

I would like to suggest that this initial step – the assertion of difference, that "this is not me, this is not mine, not my gaze, not my desire, not my story," – has been a fundamental and necessary first step for feminism. It was the recognition of, and insistence on, difference that enabled early feminist critics to focus on the difficulties faced by female authors. Similarly, feminist film theorists were able to assert that women's identification with film might be different from men's. To label this a first step is in no way intended to minimize its radical importance. Its effect can be, in fact it *has been*, enormous. Already systems both in the academy and in society at large – systems that had appeared universal, unshakable, even eternal – have been shaken.

It is the second step, however, which has proved more difficult to negotiate. The step taken by some French feminists towards essentialism – the invocation of an eternal feminine essence which has escaped culture, history, and patriarchy – seems to have led to a logical and tactical dead-end. By insisting that there is something essentially feminine outside phallocentric discourse, Irigaray runs the risk of merely reinscribing the feminine back into its original position of powerlessness, marginality, silence, and inescapable difference.[11] And the proclamation of woman's essential difference from the universal norm of "man" may merely create a new monadic universality, this time "woman," paying no heed to differences within that new unity.[12] All too often such a move only works to appropriate and deny difference. As Judith Butler points out, "There is the political problem that feminism encounters in the assumption that the term *women* denotes a common identity. Rather than a stable signifier that commands the assent of those whom it purports to describe and represent, *women*, even in the plural, has become a troublesome term, a site of contest, a cause for anxiety ... If one 'is' a woman, that is surely not all one is" (*Gender* 3).

The term "essentialism" has become almost exclusively pejorative. But, as Naomi Schor argues in "French Feminism is a Universalism," no matter how hard Butler and other feminists have tried to subvert "what has remained most stubbornly immovable ...: the idea of the universal female subject,"[13] others, in the interests of political pragmatism and other motives, have returned to and continue to utilize assertions of difference and universalism. I find this neither surprising nor lamentable. As long as women are perceived as a group and are discriminated against as a group, then it is advantageous, even imperative, that we recognize ourselves as part of that group. We have not yet arrived at the time when women's wages equal those of men or when women are free from sexual assault on the streets or in their homes. It would appear, then, that terms such as "difference" and "universal female subject," troublesome as they might be, are words and concepts whose potential has yet to be exhausted. The question then becomes whether a term like difference still has relevance for feminist reading theory.[14]

RESISTING THE TEXT

Early feminist theory relied on the theory of difference to articulate its position. Writers like Sandra Gilbert and Susan Gubar, Tille Olsen, and Elaine Showalter asked how and in what ways women could claim "authority" of their own, could "master" language, voice, and pen which had been defined as masculine.[15] Others were asking the same kinds of questions about reading. Judith Fetterley was one of the first to sound the call. In *The Resisting Reader*, Fetterley argues that women have, by and large, learned to read as men: "To read the canon of what is currently considered classic American literature is," she argues, "perforce to identify as male" (xii). Fetterley, like Irigaray, sees women as having overidentified with and through men. The corrective which she would apply is the assertion of difference. She urges the feminist critic to become a "resisting rather than an assenting reader" in order that we might "begin the process of exorcising the male mind that has been implanted in us" (xxii).

Fetterley's vigorous call is weakened by the same essentialism that we encountered in the work of Irigaray. Surely, to conceive of patriarchal ideology as a unified and malignant growth preying on the pure and virtuous female consciousness is naïve.[16] Such an assertion undermines Fetterley's otherwise energetic and astute argument. As soon as difference is asserted, there seems to be a temptation to overpolarize, to posit some entire and substantive essence that has survived behind and beyond history and culture.

Fetterley's call for a resisting reader is a call for a hypervigilant reader, alert to the dangers of seduction (in this case by the male mind). Seduction is a form of movement or displacement. To be seduced is to be moved from one's place, not exactly against one's will, but perhaps against one's better judgment. The resisting reader who refuses seduction is *always* saying, or is ready to say, "This is not me, this is not mine." Such a reading position would, it seems to me, prove both unpleasurable and unprofitable. If the reader does not allow her- or himself to be moved or seduced by the text, then the project (of reading novels at least) will be a failure. Novels *depend* upon the reader's being moved. (What we still have to find out is whether they also depend upon the heroine's being caught and arrested.) Irigaray claimed that woman placed herself in the realm of male desire through identification and implied that such a move was done in bad faith, that she would be better served by not engaging in "vicarious" or "proxy" relationships. But is there any other way to read a novel?

Fetterley's book was published in 1978. At about the same time (1975) Laura Mulvey's highly influential "Visual Pleasure and Narrative Cinema" presented an analagous argument.[17] Mulvey contended that film is structured in such a way that the viewer as "bearer of the look" is implicated into a masculine and even sadistic way of looking, that – through camera shots, point of view, and editing – our gaze is routed through the probing, aggressive view of the camera. We can, it was argued, apprehend the heroine in no other way: "Cinema builds the way she is to be looked at into the spectacle itself" (25). Fetterley had argued that we must try to resist the masculine gaze that was foisted on us in literature; Mulvey seemed to imply that such resistance was futile, that our gaze was, as it were, written into the script (*and* the camera angle, *and* the editing, etc.).

Mulvey's thesis had substantial impact. Feminist theorists of film, art, and culture used her insight in their critiques of the representation of the female form to show how its framing already encoded woman as a passive sexual object available for our viewing pleasure. Teresa de Lauretis, for example, argues in *Alice Doesn't* that this polarization (between active, masculine gaze and passive, feminine object) is inextricably woven into all narrative which offers only the "two mythical positions of hero (mythical subject) and boundary (spatially fixed object, personified obstacle)" (123). The first is obviously masculine, the second feminine. In "The Violence of Rhetoric" de Lauretis takes this argument further: "For the subject of violence is always, by definition, masculine; 'man' is by definition the subject of culture and of any social act" (250). In *Alice Doesn't*, following Greimas, she argues that *all* narrative is structured by "the movement of the actant subject toward an actant-object" and, that the actant subject is always and absolutely construed as male (112). In other words, even if a woman were to act in such a role, she would be acting *as* a man. She would be taking the male role in the narrative. De Lauretis' compelling argument is that the structure of narrative is consistently sexually differentiated and differentiating.

A thesis such as Mulvey's is influential to the degree to which it can be productively applied to a wide range of texts, and indeed it does seem to work for the four early novels considered here. These novels, which I have said both portray and teach correct emotional response, depict primarily *male* response. Again and again the stories shift away from what would seem to be their primary focus (the suffering heroine) onto the struggles, rivalries, and bonds between the male characters. Cousin Morden hunts Lovelace down and kills him, while Belford is reformed. Chillingworth seeks Dimmesdale's secret; the two men's lives become unhealthily entwined. Lord Warburton, Ralph Touchett, and Caspar Goodwood draw closer to each other in their appreciation of and sympathy for Isabel Archer. Angel Clare and Alec d'Urberville act as doubles and rivals in their attempts to possess and love Tess. In each case, the drama shifts from one centred on the trials and troubles of a single female character to one involving only men. When we turn to the work of Atwood and Carter, we will consider the extent to which this continues to be true.

What is the significance of this male clustering? What, particularly, does it mean for the female reader? Could it be that since our response as readers is routed primarily through these male characters, then we must all, male or female, "apprehend" the heroine through the male gaze and male vision? This would mean, following Mulvey's lead, that our pleasure depends upon the heroine's pain, that ours is a desire for her destruction, that we readers got a voyeuristic and even sadistic thrill out of seeing Clarissa and her sisters suffer. Although the argument is compelling and goes far in helping us understand the gender politics structuring these novels, it does not go far enough.

There are several problems with such a view of readers and heroines. The first is its polarization and oversimplification of subject positions: only two roles are available, in the case of these novels, passive female victim or active male viewer/sadist. Mulvey's description of spectatorial/reader positions allows no room for oppositional positions; it assumes that we are all held transfixed without the ability (or perhaps even the desire) to see, to read, or to feel differently. A number of theorists have commented on this weakness. Gay and lesbian theorists, in particular, have noted that their identifications and desires do not always follow such pre-scribed trajectories.[18]

IDENTITIES AND IDENTIFICATIONS

It is probably advisable at this point to consider the differences and the connections between the terms "identity" and "identification." Our identity, simply put, is who we think we are, who we *tell* our-selves we are or ought to be. To some extent this identity is usually based on race, class, ethnicity, gender and sexual orientation. But these factors can be restrictive and are not sufficient in themselves to account for who we are. As Judith Butler put it, "If one 'is' a woman, that is surely not all one is." We do not want our gender to prescribe who we are or can be. We want to make sure that in our rush to claim our difference we do not blunder into another sameness. Neither do we want, however, to deny the politically pragmatic and necessary allegiance to feminism.

In her 1989 *Essentially Speaking*, Diana Fuss addresses this prob-lem: "At no other time in the history of feminist theory has identi-ty been at once so vilified and so sanctified; there is no middle ground, it seems, on the question" (102). The problem, as she sees it, has come about because of our insistence on "locating difference outside identity, in the spaces between identities" which "ignore[s] the radicality of the poststructuralist view which locates differences within identity" (103). Working from both Foucault's definition of a subject as a position that may be filled in certan conditions by various individuals,[19] and Gayatri Spivak's theory of subject posi-tions, Fuss begins to sketch out a theory of reading that visualizes "the subject as a site of multiple and heterogeneous differences" and "the 'I' as a complicated field of multiple subjectivities and competing identities" (33). Thus she offers us a way to hold on to the philosophically and politically useful concept of difference with-out inviting the collapse into essentialism.

Lacan's model of subjectivity might allow us to sketch what "difference within" might mean. For Lacan, the subject is structured around a gap that is fundamental and unbridgeable.[20] This begins in the mirror stage when the young subject perceives a difference between its coherent representation in the mirror and the disorganized self it feels itself to be, between its own perceived inadequacy and the apparent coherence of the figure it sees. "The mirror stage," writes Lacan, "is a drama whose internal thrust is precipitated from insufficiency to anticipation" (4). The subject, feeling itself to be insufficient, is attracted by its mirror image and anticipates a fuller identity as that image, an identity it can never achieve.

If we are to believe Lacan, our sense of ourselves as subjects is predicated on this fundamental split. The very fact that we feel ourselves to be an "I" at all is based on our recognition of the "not I." Difference is, as it were, already written into our identity. As mentioned above, the Laplanche and Pontalis definition of identification is "the psychological process whereby *the subject* assimilates an aspect, property or attribute of the other and *is transformed*, wholly or partially, after the model the other provides."

Identity is the *fiction* of the cohesive, autonomous self. The irony is that this autonomous "I" should be built out of identifications with the "not I." Identity and identification seem to work against each other, for as Judith Butler puts it, "Identifications ... unsettle the 'I'; they are the sedimentation of the 'we' in the constitution of any 'I'" (*Bodies* 105). In *Identification Papers*, Diana Fuss writes: "While we tend to experience our identities as part of our public personas ... we experience our identifications as more private, guarded, evasive" (2). She sees identification as something which disturbs and disrupts identity "even as it makes possible the formation of an *illusion of identity*." "Identification," she concludes, "is the detour through the other that defines a self" (2).

MASOCHISM AND SYMPATHY – THE "FEMININE" ATTACHMENTS

The identifications offered us in the novels considered here permit a dizzying array of detours. According to Mulvey's theory all readers, male and female, must identify with, and read through, the heroines' male admirers. While this accounts for some of the routes of identification constructed in the novels, it fails to encompass others. For instance, how do we explain the cross-gender identification involved in the way male characters (Lovelace, Dimmesdale, Ralph Angel, etc.) "feel through" and identify with their heroines? Mulvey might say that by allying ourselves with the male admirers we are safely on the side of the sadistic, cool and controlling gaze of the camera or author, but I wonder whether in identifying with our heroine, we readers are not putting ourselves (gloriously, heroically) at risk by sharing her pain and using it as the cornerstone, the bedrock, of our aesthetic pleasure. It seems that ours is nothing so simple as a sadistic desire. Instead, I will be arguing that we are driven by *twinned* desires: the first a desire to "have" the heroine, to use her as an empty vehicle through which we can feel (this is perhaps close to Mulvey's sadism) and the other the desire to "be" the heroine – to experience, through her, the powers *and* dangerous pleasures of her helpless and yet seductive position. If this is so, if these are indeed the twinned desires which connect us to the heroine, then the desire that is constructed for us in the novels is as masochistic as it is sadistic.

Jessica Benjamin asked how it has come to be that femininity should be linked to passivity and even masochism. Carol Siegel addresses this question in the introduction to her book, *Male Masochism: Modern Revisions of the Story of Love*. While she acknowledges that "in popular culture masochism is associated with femininity" (2), she demonstrates that it has not always been so (10–17). Medieval troubadours and Renaissance poets, she claims, declared themselves slaves to their loves, and only in the latter half of the nineteenth century would a man declaring such emotion risk appearing emasculated: "After Freud, the lover's willingness to cast himself at the feet of his mistress is read as a perverse total renunciation of masculinity. And the lover's every reiteration of his limitless subjection to woman is interpreted as an unconscious revelation of homosexuality" (10). Siegel does not lay all the blame for such a view on Freud himself but sees it as a response to increasing feminist activity and increasing female power in the latter half of the nineteenth century. Man felt threatened and could no longer "play" at being subservient. Even the lover's subordination to his mistress was potentially threatening. She writes of the "fearful reversal [which] can result from the supposedly emasculating power of love, which threatens to reduce man to a sentimental and therefore womanly emotional state" (8). Such sentiment and such emotion can lead to a loss of self and is therefore seen as threatening to one's masculinity, one's sense of autonomous selfhood. According to Siegel, it is not so much that femininity is drawn to masochism as that masochism has been pathologized and labelled feminine(1–22).

An interesting parallel to Siegel's analysis is offered by Diana Fuss in *Identification Papers*. There she argues that Freud developed the theory of identification as a "corrective" to nineteenth-century ideas about sympathy. She claims that Freud denigrated sympathy in much the same way, and on the same grounds, as he did masochism. Each was seen as suspiciously feminine, involving a threatening loss of self. Fuss writes: "Freud presents his theory of psychical identification specifically as a corrective to the figurative excesses of nineteenth-century psychology. Identification replaces 'sympathy,' 'imagination,' and 'suggestion' to describe in more 'scientific' fashion, the phenomenon of how subjects act upon one another" (4). She continues: "Freud's later work seeks to replace the nineteenth-cantury notion of 'sympathy' with a more rigorous and modern theory of 'identification' ... These theoretical categories are completely gender-inflected: an 'emotion' not a 'mechanism,' sympathy comes under suspicion as a peculiarly feminine attribute. By the time of Group Psychology, Freud understands identification as a phallicizing process (the erection of the ego) that must be firmly distinguished from the feminizing emotion of sympathy (the splitting or diffusion of the ego)" (114). The firm, the scientific, the *masculine* identification thus comes to have precedence over its weaker and sillier, tender-hearted sister, sympathy.

Both sympathy and masochism involve an identification with pain. Leo Bersani writes, "'Sympathy' always includes a trace of sexual pleasure [which] is ... inescapably masochistic ... There is a certain risk in all sympathetic projections ... a secret attachment to scenes of suffering and violence"(*Representation* 150). I would like to trace some of the connections between these terms and the gendered associations they evoke.

EMPATHETIC APPETITES

We continue to view sympathy and empathy as female traits. Empathy has recently been claimed by feminists as an emotion of their own. Judith Kegan Gardiner states that "empathy in twentieth-century Western culture has become a specially marked female trait"

(2). Gardiner bases her argument on the work of Nancy Chodorow and other contemporary American psychoanalysts. She writes that Nancy Chodorow claims that girls, hence women, "have a basis for 'empathy' built into their primary definition of self in a way that boys do not."[21] One problem with a claim such as Gardiner's is the degree to which empathy is presented as an unproblematic and ultimately positive response.

Stephen Greenblatt, in *Renaissance Self-Fashioning*, provides us with a somewhat different view. He writes of empathy being "deployed" during the Renaissance and the age of exploration as a mechanism of *power*, as a means of wresting control from those who were apprehended and pitied. In this view, empathy becomes not so much a "tender" feminine response as much as (nearly always masculine) tool of aggression. He sees "modern man" as using improvisation and "psychic mobility" (the ability to understand others and perform their roles, act as they do) to encounter and ultimately conquer other civilizations (224). He cites Daniel Lerner's assessment of Western society as highly adaptable and responsive to new cultures and new demands. Lerner calls this capacity to see oneself in another's place "empathy," but Greenblatt warns that we are misled if we believe that empathy is simply "an act of imaginative generosity, a sympathetic appreciation of the situation of the other fellow" (227). He goes on: "What is most disturbing ... is that the imagined self-loss [in empathy] conceals its opposite: a ruthless displacement and absorption of the other. Empathy, as the German *Einfühlung* suggests, may be a feeling of oneself into an object [sic], but that object may have to be drained of its own substance before it will serve as an appropriate vessel" (236).

It seems to me that this view of empathy is very close to the notion I want to construct. Greenblatt refers to empathy as a tool whereby one culture may be "displaced and absorbed" by another. I would argue that it is the figure of the heroine as victim which is displaced and absorbed in the reading process. Like the object of *Einfühlung*, she must be drained of her own substance before serving "as an appropriate vessel" for our own emotion and pity. Our full empathetic response depends upon her empty passivity; it can only be constructed out of her emptiness and her pain. What more appropriate vessel than the already drained Clarissa or Tess, the woman as nothing out of which meaning is made?

Fuss also notes the connection between "identification" and colonialism. She writes: "Identification is neither a historically universal concept nor a politicaly innocent one. A by-product of modernity, the psychoanalytic theory of identification takes shape within the larger cultural context of colonial expansion and imperial crisis" (*Identification* 141–2).

To help us thread our way through this maze of identifications and sympathetic and empathetic relations, I turn now to the work of Georges Poulet. In his 1969 "Phenomenology of Reading" Poulet provides a fable, instructive in the mores of reading, power and seduction. His is an extraordinarily sensitive account of his own reader response. Of particular note here is Poulet's insistence upon, and exaggeration of, the shifting power and gender positions taken by the reader. He sees himself now as victorious hero-rescuer, and now as victim or prey. These shifts, which are presented as the result of being "moved" by pity, sympathy, or empathy, seem to depend upon a "drained" and feminized spectacle.

Poulet begins by musing on the objectness of books, a state which rouses his pity: "When I see them on display, I look at them as I would at animals for sale, kept in little cages, and so obviously hoping for a buyer"(53). Although Poulet's explicit analogy is between books and animals, I am struck by the *unexpressed* analogy to women on display. These books are like Sleeping Beauties waiting to be rescued by the prince (in this case, a lowly reader): "On a table, on bookshelves, in store windows, they wait for someone to come and deliver them from their materiality, from their immobility ... Made of paper and ink, they lie where they are put, until the moment some one shows an interest in them. They wait. Are they aware that an act of man might suddenly transform their existence? They appear to be lit up with that hope. Read me, they seem to say. I find it hard to resist their appeal. No, books are not just objects among others" (53).

These books seem more like prostitutes on the street corner, wallflowers at a school dance, or heroines in romantic novels than animals for sale in a pet shop window. Poulet's empathy is aroused by what he sees as the tragedy of subjects caught in object-hood. This particular conjunction stirs and emboldens him until he is unable to "resist their appeal." It allows him to imagine himself as transformer, life-giver, hero. As reader he is active, free, and a potential rescuer. The books, in contrast, lie mute, on display and somehow ashamed of their objectified status. In Greenblatt's terms, it would seem to be the extent to which they are drained of their "own substance" (subjectivity) that allows them to "serve as appropriate vessels" for the reader's emotional investment. They lie like the jewels of the Orient, or the forests of the New World, ready to be "appreciated" and consumed by the empathetic appetite.

The only power granted to the books is that of seduction. Theirs is the seduction of pathos, a seduction based on helplessness and humility. Like the heroines in *Clarissa*, *Scarlet Letter*, *Portrait of a Lady*, and *Tess of the d'Urbervilles*, unable to move themselves, they can depend only upon their ability to move others. As readers lured toward these objectified, pathetic texts, we experience growing feelings of potency, a potency created in response to the books' apparent impotence. What this would imply is that one subject's power depends upon the representation of another's powerlessness, that one feels oneself most free and most powerful when confronted with one who is not free.

In Poulet's account, however, the reader's active and heroic position is not maintained. He suggests later in the same article that it is the reader who is under bondage to the book: "I deliver myself, bound hand and foot, to the omnipotence of fiction ... I become the prey of language. There is no escaping this take-over" (55). What is so remarkable about this statement is the extreme nature of the switch. The reader who was so activized, heroicized, and masculinized as rescuer, is now feminized, victimized – a masochist. This switch from one role to another is, as I shall hope to show in my study of other texts, fairly common. The reader who, in one sense is made powerful by his or her sympathy with the heroine as victim, runs the risk of over-identification, of getting "infected" by her powerlessness and victimization.

I will be arguing in the coming chapters that we, as readers are subjected to twin and contradictory directives. On one hand, we are roused to action, made to feel heroic (masculinized?) in the face of our heroine's plight. On the other hand, our very identification with her and her seductive powers renders us helpless, infects us with a lassitude, a sense of helpless impotence. This second narrative thread disempowers as the first empowers.

This is the paradox: that the reader should be both roused to action and full subjectivity by the spectacle of female suffering *and* made passive and unable to feel except through the agency of others. According to Poulet: "Reading, then, is the act in which the subjective principle which I call *I*, is modified in such a way that I no longer have the right, strictly speaking, to consider it as my *I*. I am on loan to another, and this other thinks, feels, suffers, and acts within me" (57). Reading is the act in which one finds – only to lose – oneself, in which one feels "on loan to another" who "thinks, feels, suffers, and acts within me."

The novels' social work is the creation of this subject-effect. But what sort of subjectivity is constituted by this suspension of self, this sense that I am both myself and another? We feel the proximity of a subject and are initially confused. What is it that we feel? Where does this feeling come from? Does it come from the hero/ine, the author, ourselves? To whom are we responding when we read? This confusion of roles, the sense that we cannot tell ourselves from the character or the author is what we call identification. Flaubert said of his heroine, "Madame Bovary, c'est moi," and Poulet quotes Rimbaud, "Je est un autre" (57).²² The confusion is, I believe, as productive as it is unresolvable.

The novel is the "place" where consciousness is created for us to possess, to colonize, and to empathize (with). It is the place in which our own emotions are produced and designed through sympathy and identification. The reader changes places, assumes roles of both sexes, plays at being hero, plays at being victim. The figure of the heroine victim activates a certain *sort* of identification. She becomes a "charge" or a "field of emotional power" through which readers re-charge themselves. The feminist critic both enters this field to experience the identifications first hand *and* watches from the outside to see how the paths and routes of identification are constructed, noting the power different positions produce.

2 *Clarissa*: Novel as Trial

In volume 1 of *Clarissa*, Clarissa Harlowe's uncle writes to her: "Everybody loves you ... But how can we resolve to see you? There is no standing against your looks and language ... For my part, I could not read your letter to me, without being unmanned. How can you be so unmoved yourself, yet be so able to move everybody else?" (1:304). Alarmed by the intensity of the response that Clarissa generates, her uncle seeks to check it by holding her at arm's length, refusing to see her or to read her letters. He is afraid of her ability to move him. Clarissa – like all the heroine victims studied in this book – may be unable to move on her own, but she is *intensely* capable of moving others. It is this capacity to move both characters and us, the readers, that makes her a heroine. In order to study such a heroine, therefore, we need to look not so much at what she does, as at our own response, at the way she "moves" us.

Although it may appear that Uncle Harlowe is overreacting in not allowing Clarissa into his sight for fear of losing his composure, the novel would teach us that he is not. He worries that a close encounter will "unman" him, that in letting himself love her he will lose his own sense of self. In one sense his reaction is depicted as extreme and even unjust, but we are, I believe, meant to take seriously the potency of Clarissa's effects. She is a figure who must be approached cautiously; her power is real. When the uncle says he fears being unmanned, we are reminded that by loving her we might lose our sense of ourselves as separate and autonomous subjects and that in feeling the effects of her tragic female power, we might be infected by it.[1] What the novel attempts to teach is how to approach and love her without sacrificing any of our own integrity. It may be that she has to be held and "arrested" in order that we may keep our own identity, our sense of active subjectivity, alive. This may be the only way we are able to feel her power and not get scorched by it. Frozen as the fixed object of our investigative eye, she is held so that we are free to investigate, probe and know her. This makes it easier for us to examine her sexuality, her will, and her desire and not be "unmanned" or disarmed in the process. We are able to retain (or create) our own sense of agency and power out of her arrest. Our masculinized agency depends upon her feminized passivity. This process of arrest and examination is called a trial.

In the second volume of *Clarissa* Lovelace writes to Belford that "a trial seems necessary for the *further* establishment of the honour of so excellent a creature [Clarissa]" (2:40). This statement could equally well stand as the project of the novel as a whole. The novel is an extended trial – an exploration or putting to the test – of Clarissa's honor.[2] This chapter will be a consideration of *Clarissa* as a type of trial or theatre of punishment. Clarissa is the star of this trial or theatre, the object of our attention and our gaze.

In *The Rise of the Novel*, Ian Watt, having explored analogies between philosophy and literature, turns to "another group of specialists in epistemology, the jury in a court of law. Their expectations, and those of the novel reader coincide," he claims, "in many ways" (31). Watt sees the reader's position – spectatorial, democratic, and judgmental – as being analogous to a juror's. While I believe that this insight is fundamentally correct, it seems to me that the reader's position is more problematic and less secure than Watt suggests, that once the reader enters the theatre of punishment, he or she is implicated through identification into positions of both innocence and guilt, becoming at once prisoner *and* judge. This chapter will explore the consequence for the reader of such identifications and will question how these positions of innocence and guilt, prisoner and judge, disturb and/or construct gender.

Clarissa is a novel obsessed with the problems of judgment. Its language is suffused with the vocabulary of trial and courtroom. Not surprisingly perhaps, a similar language has permeated the responses of its readers. Diderot "tried" his friends by their reaction to Richardson's novels: "They [the novels] have become my touchstones; those who are displeased by them are judged for me."[3] A more recent controversy has continued to use the same language. Terry Castle sees Clarissa as an "exemplary victim" of hermeneutic violence, and argues in her defense because, as she sees it, Clarissa's "is that voice which repeatedly fails to make itself heard" on its own (22). William Warner, on the other hand, feels that it is Lovelace who needs to be defended against the artful Clarissa and all those critics who, he feels, have condemned him so unjustly. Terry Eagleton turns on the critics who he says have tried "to convict" Clarissa and argues that "even when the most damning evidence [against her] has been gleefully summoned for the prosecution, it remains on balance, remarkably feeble" (71–2).

These comments are striking in two ways. First, the critics are responding as if the characters were real people.[4] The second striking feature – connected to the first – is that readers seem to feel a strong need to defend and to accuse. That readers are frequently "pulled into" Clarissa in an immediate and startling way has been noted on many occasions.[5] What I would like to point out is that these readers so frequently seem to get pulled into "judgmental" positions. They plunge into the text to blame or to defend, to vindicate or to accuse. This may be a novel that demands our participation, but we still need to ascertain what role the reader is expected to play in this courtroom of emotion. Are we to be judge or witness, victim or executioner? Finally we are led to wonder about the role of gender in all of this, for it certainly seems that it was as much sexual politics as literary insight that pulled Castle, Eagleton, and Warner into the fray, and that made their polemics on Clarissa so attractive and relevant to a contemporary audience.

Readers drawn into such positions are not experiencing identification as we would define it in the late twentieth century. They do not, after all, feel so much that they *are* Clarissa or that they *become* Lovelace as they feel called upon to defend and to accuse these characters. Neither do readers seem to feel that they have to take a position which is consistently pro Clarissa or pro Lovelace; in fact, some inconsistency or "play" in allegiance is desirable (for this is how gender is constructed). We move back and forth between captive and captor, between masculinity and femininity.[6] What *is* essential is that the reader enter in some way into the play of judgment and sympathy which provides the novel with both its form and its content. The reader enters into this play by assuming various roles of the courtroom.

In order to give the terms theatre and trial full consideration, in order to appreciate the connections and the tensions between the two, we need to make a detour into some eighteenth-century thought on "theatricality." I have referred to *Clarissa* as both a trial and a *theatre* of punishment. The connection between these two arenas was disturbingly close for some writers in the eighteenth century.

The trial is usually conceived of as the place where truth is revealed and discovered. Its very existence is based on the premise that such truth is *not* self-evident, obvious, or on display. It is only through the accumulation of evidence, acute observation, and objective analysis that truth can be produced. The subject who acts as judge in a trial relies on detachment and objectivity and must not become emotionally involved with the object on trial. He (the position has traditionally been a masculine one) is active, vigilant, and aggressive in his search for truth.

The theatre, in contrast, is involved with illusion and fantasy. That which it displays is apprehended not so much through reason, logic, and argument as through emotional involvement and visual display. In this case the subject who watches, as opposed to the subject who judges in a trial, is passive and lets him- or herself be moved by, and emotionally involved with, the spectacle presented. When one is "moved," "seduced," or "enthralled" in this way, one gives up one's identity to the other, loses one's own sense of self in feeling for the other. This type of relationship between spectator and spectacle troubled eighteenth-century thinkers such as Diderot, Rousseau and Bernard Mandeville. They worried that the passions were lured too easily into sympathy, love, pity, or hate, that the eye could too easily be tricked or deceived.

It is this response to the theatre that Michael Fried analyzes in his *Absorption and Theatricality*. There he writes of the prevailing distrust of anything or anyone who courted the beholder's attention (103). This distrust was based on the belief that virtue lay in appearing neither to pander to nor in any way solicit the regard (in both the French and the English senses) of another. To put oneself on display or to show oneself became a kind of degradation akin to prostitution. This extreme distrust of anything that courted the gaze led, Fried claims, to the paradox that "it was only by negating the beholder's presence" that a painting could in fact claim the attention of the viewer (103). A work of art gained value by seeming to be oblivious to its own "theatricality," to the fact that is was produced to be admired. The paradox is that viewers or spectators would be drawn toward and come to value works that denied their own existence. The spectator or viewer would have to enter into a kind of aesthetic contract with the artist and become an accomplice to the illusion that the work was never intended to be seen: "But it seems clear that starting around the middle of the eighteenth century in France the beholder's presence before the painting came increasingly to be conceived by critics and theorists as something that had to be accomplished or at least powerfully affirmed by the painting itself; and more generally that the existence of the beholder, which is to say the primordial convention that paintings are made to be beheld, emerged as problematic for painting as never before" (93). Fried demonstrates that this reaction to painting was but one aspect of a widely based distrust of all spectacle-spectator relations.

One of the strongest examples of anti-theatrical writing of this time is Rousseau's *Letter to M. d'Alembert on the Theatre*. Led by his belief in the danger and power of spectacle, Rousseau urges the citizens of Geneva not to open a theatre which, he argues, could only corrupt. For Rousseau an actor is hollow because, in the process of emptying himself out to play another, he has lost possession of himself, has offered himself up to the other (80–1). Acting, he writes, "is a trade in which [the actor] performs for money, submits himself to the disgrace and the affronts that others buy the right to give him, and puts his person publicly on sale" (79). The actor then, as described by Rousseau, is essentially a prostitute. Not only does acting degrade by making actors appear to sell themselves; there are other sexual disturbances as well. To act, Rousseau hints, is in some sense to feminize and thereby disgrace the self.[7] This is a kind of double move wherein Rousseau first disgraces actors by calling them womanly and then insults women by referring to them as actors. (The latter charge would probably carry less weight since women were already held to be inherently duplicitous and fickle.[8])

Drawing on the same sense of distrust, Denis Diderot attempted to establish new aesthetic criteria that would temper the morally ambivalent theatrical relations between spectator and spectacle in painting and drama. In his art criticism, he praised paintings whose subjects did not appear to solicit the spectator's gaze. The paintings that he admired typically represented a subject (most often female) absorbed in reverie. This figure, who did not look at the viewer, would in no way acknowledge his presence (and in most cases the coy suggestiveness of the scenes could only imply a male viewer). The paradoxical result, as Fried states, was "that Diderot's conception of painting rested ultimately upon the supreme fiction that the beholder did not exist" (103).

In drama this view manifested itself in Diderot's famous advice to playwrights and actors that they should envision a fourth wall separating them from their audience: "Whether you compose or act, think no more of the beholder than if he did not exist. Imagine, at the edge of the stage, a high wall that separates you from the orchestra. Act as if the curtain never rose."[9] The best acting, in other words, results when actors act as if they are not acting. The best drama (and painting) should not appear to have been designed and plotted for us to see. The effect should be that we just happen to come across these scenes as if by accident. This aesthetic creed has prevailed to a great extent in all narrative art, including drama and the novel, to the present day.[10]

In painting, drama, and society at large, thinkers such as Rousseau and Diderot tried to warn against the moral threat of theatricality. What was it that worried them so? Rousseau distrusted the actor and thought that his attempts to win applause and attention threatened his autonomy, "fullness," and self-possession, all, it seems to me, equivalents of masculinity. That *need* for recognition by the other, in Rousseau's view, weakened an individual's ability to be self-sufficient and thereby feminized him.

If thinkers such as Rousseau worried that spectators had to protect themselves against the enticement of spectacle in order to preserve their integrity and autonomy, Adam Smith in *The Theory of Moral Sentiments* (1759) speculated about the role which sympathy might play in *bridging* the distance between such autonomous individuals. Like Rousseau and Diderot he couched his argument in theatrical terms. Unlike Rousseau and Diderot, however, Smith uses terms that seem gender neutral (or is it that they are consistently uni-sexual and thus masculine by default?).

Sympathy, for Smith, is in itself an inherently theatrical relation because it depends upon the sufferer's being able to represent his or her pain in such a way that the other may recognize it and respond accordingly. The pain or distress must be *displayed* if it is to be acknowledged. Similarly, if sympathy is to be performed correctly, the one who watches must also seek to attune his or her own reaction to the sufferer. As David Marshall puts it, "For Smith, sympathy depends upon a theatrical relation between a spectator and spectacle, a relation that is reversed and mirrored as both persons try to represent the other's feelings."[11] In other words, there can be no sympathy without a code of conventions, signals whereby we can read each others' distress. Even at that, Smith wonders how it is that we can ever claim to experience the pain of another: "Though our brother is upon the rack, as long as we ourselves are at our ease, our senses will never inform us of what he suffers"(9). He concludes that our capacity for imagination is responsible for allowing us access to the sensory life of another: "By imagination we place ourselves in his situation, we conceive ourselves enduring all the same torments, we enter as it were into his body, and become in some measure the same person with him" (3). This transfer or exchange of our own state for another's, taking place through the agency of imagination, sounds remarkably like the transfer that takes place in reading. For Smith, however, the act is not so much aesthetic as social: "this is the source of our fellow-feeling for the misery of others ... It is by changing places in fancy with the sufferer, that we come either to conceive or to be affected by what he feels" (3). David Marshall sees this social vision of Smith's as a kind of dream or fiction because Smith "can't believe ... that fellow-feeling is automatic or even natural" (180). He goes on: "*The Theory of Moral Sentiments*, then, must describe what it is like to want to believe in the fiction of sympathy, and what it's like to live in a world where sympathy is perhaps impossible" (181). If we accept Marshall's assessment of Smith's vision of sympathy as an unrealizable dream, we might see the work of the novel as an agency which fosters that dream, keeps the fantasy alive.[12]

One reason that Adam Smith is relevant to a discussion of *Clarissa* is that while other eighteenth-century writers tend to picture the passions as a threat to judgment, Smith sees sympathy itself as a kind of judgment. Both of these views – that there is a danger in being moved because sympathy tends to trick reason and that sympathy is the highest form of judgment – paradoxical and yet twinned, are explored in, and lie at the heart of, *Clarissa*.

I have discussed the eighteenth-century issues of theatricality and sympathy at some length because they provide the context within which I can place my own study of the reader's position in *Clarissa*. The theatre was threatening to Diderot and Rousseau because of the apparent sexual and power relations between actors and audience. They saw the spectacle as a form of seduction, the actor as a type of salesman or prostitute, and the spectator as a dupe. The theatre was the place in which the spectator *willingly* lost his or her own sense of self and in which actors lost their autonomy and self-possession. Such an imagined loss is the basis for Clarissa's uncle's fear of seeing her in person: "There is no standing against your looks and language." To be moved by her plight would be to become "unmanned."[13]

It is in part because of such power that Richardson is careful to establish the reader's place in his novel so as to maximize sympathy and as far as possible avoid the dangers of theatricality. To do so, he relies on the conventions of the trial as a sort of antidote, or regulatory check on the theatre. The question that remains, however, is to what extent the trial is already "infected" with theatre, with – that is – the political and erotic lure of the spectacle. Can the trial prevent us from being unmanned? Or does the trial merely set new parameters for the construction of gender?

In order to demonstrate the way in which the text guides us to our proper place and fixes us in our position of spectatorship (whether in theater or courtroom), I will begin with the opening letter from Anna Howe to Clarissa: "I am extremely concerned, my dearest friend, for the disturbances that have happened in your family. I know how it must hurt you to become the subject of the public talk; and yet upon an occasion so generally known, it is impossible but that whatever relates to a young lady, whose distinguished merits have made her the public care, should engage everybody's attention" (1:1).

This passage establishes (at least) three things. The first is that Clarissa is an object of interest, one worthy of our attention. Not only is she "distinguished," but she "*should* engage *everybody's* attention" (my own emphasis). The use of "should" and "everybody" as well as the earlier "it is impossible" establish a mildly regulatory tone, a normative pressure on the reader to conform.

The establishment of Clarissa as an object of interest is compulsively repeated in subsequent paragraphs. There, it is presented in the frame of concerned gossip: "Mr Diggs, the surgeon ... *told me*," "Mr Wyerley drank tea with us yesterday; and ... both he and Mr Symmes *blame*," "They *say*," "This I am *told*," "There are people who love not your brother ... these *say*" (1:1; all the emphases are my own). The effect of these repetitions, these "they say"s and "he told me"s, is to demarcate a circle of gossip and attention within which characters – Clarissa, a brother, a family, and Lovelace – begin to appear. Such markers function like the dimming lights and lifting curtain in the theatre. Their function is to distinguish, to mark off or frame, certain individuals and certain attitudes as worthy of our attention.[14]

The second point established in this passage is that to be "the subject of the public talk ... must hurt." Why this should be so is explained on the next page: "So desirous, as you always said, of sliding through life to the end of it unnoted; and, as I may add, not wishing to be observed even for your silent benevolence ... *Rather useful than glaring*, your deserved motto; though now to your regret, pushed into blaze" (1:2) It is essential for the establishment of Clarissa's virtue that she be presented as wanting to slide through life unnoticed. A reluctance to be on display is perhaps the defining feature of her virtue. "But I will not," she declares, "if I can help it, be made a show of; especially to men of whose characters and principles I have no good opinion" (1:212). Again after her rape, she pleads with Lovelace to send her to Bedlam if he must, but begs, "Don't let me be made a show of" (2:212). Even after her death, her will declares that "it is my desire that I may not be unnecessarily exposed to the view of anybody," and she is especially concerned that Lovelace "might not be allowed to see my corpse" (4:416).

It is as if to show herself would be bad enough, but to show herself to men of bad character and especially, therefore, to Lovelace would be to risk a special kind of degradation. This is why the text is so careful only to allow us to look at her in the "right" way. It constructs us, or rather helps us to construct ourselves, as readers of "characters and principles" of which Clarissa would approve. It sanctions our position as beholder and Clarissa's position as the beheld by absolving her of any charge of seeking our gaze. We may look, but we must look carefully; our gaze has the power to "hurt."

Anna's awareness of Clarissa's probable pain, evident in the phrases "must hurt" and "I am extremely concerned," creates the third effect – the establishment of sympathy for the heroine. David Marshall, in *The Surprising Effects of Sympathy*, defines sympathy as "the capacity to feel the sentiments of someone else" (3). It is that capacity which is being constructed for the reader here. Clarissa, Anna reminds us, "is the public care." The text thereby delivers her to us as an interesting object of attention, but with the admonition that we must "care." Our relationship toward her is established as one of concern and pity. We are urged to look, but only on the condition that we look and feel "correctly." Our gaze and our emotional response are coached and disciplined.

Within the first paragraph, only two sentences long, the dynamics for reading this novel have been established. The heroine, by being the "subject of the public talk," becomes the object of our attention as well. That talk and that attention will, in turn, "hurt" her. This hurt (prefiguring the further pain she will be made to endure) arouses our sympathy. Attention, pain and sympathy mark out the field the novel will explore, a field it shares with both the theatre and the courtroom.[15] The elements in this structure are neither static nor fixed. Instead, attention, pain, and sympathy circulate in a process whereby each succeeds the other and each sparks the other off in a self-perpetuating economy of punishment and pleasure.

One of the features of such a process is that just as the triad itself is not fixed, neither are the positions of the characters who act within it. No one remains solely victim or prosecutor. The roles of judge, witness, criminal, lawyer, jailer, and executioner are played by various characters in turn.[16] While Clarissa is obviously the primary victim, she is certainly not the only one. Neither is Lovelace the only villain. Roles shift in this novel. When, for example, Clarissa complains to her mother, "And here I cannot but express my grief that I should have all the punishment and all the blame" (1:117), her mother replies: "Say not all the blame and all the punishment is yours. I am as much blamed, and as much punished as you are; yet am more innocent" (1:118). Indeed, her mother is amply punished at the end of the book. She and all the family members are made to suffer enormously for the hurt they caused Clarissa.

No one gets all the punishment and all the blame in this novel. Instead, roles are played interchangeably by one character after another. Punishment and blame, innocence and guilt: characters seem to "try on" these attributes as they might clothing, and through them the readers are able to experience the same freedom, and sometimes, the same pain. Anna, for example, sees herself at varying times as judge, witness ("A stander-by may see more of the game than one who plays" [1:7], or even executioner.[17] Drawn by their theatrical possibilities, Lovelace assumes many of the roles of the courtroom. One of his favourites is witness or lawyer. He tends to dwell on the erotic and narcissistic effects of his power: "The ladies, elder and younger, had their handkerchiefs to their eyes at the just testimony which I bore to the merits of this exalted creature; and which I would ... bear at the bar of a court of justice" (3:408), and: "What an admirable lawyer should I have made and what a poor hand would this charming creature, with all her innocence, have made of it in a court of justice against a man who had so much to *say* and to *show* for himself!" (4:230–1). He is equally taken with imagining himself a prisoner. He writes to Anna Howe: "I will be content to do it [meet Clarissa] with a halter about my neck; and attended by a parson on my right hand, and the hangman on my left, be doomed, at her will, either to the church or the gallows" (3:425).

Clarissa herself, though pre-eminently the victim of this novel, also appears at different times as lawyer, judge, prosecutor, and witness. Cousin Morden acts as detective, judge, and executioner. Members of Clarissa's family are at once torturers, judges, executioners (her father's curse is the most compelling example of this), and at the end victims themselves. Readers, drawn in by the epistolary style and the rapidly changing viewpoints, are encouraged, like the characters, to move from one role to another.

I would like to consider two trial scenes in *Clarissa* which play out some of the issues of courtroom theatrics which have been discussed here. These scenes are notable for several reasons. The first is that they reverse the roles the main characters generally play in the rest of the novel. Lovelace, usually presented as jailer, torturer, or executioner, is himself on trial in the first scene. Clarissa, prisoner and victim extraordinaire, plays the role of judge in the second. These scenes are also notable for the means by which they instruct the reader on the proper way to know and to judge. Readers are invited both to identify with and at the same time to judge characters within the text. We are thereby permitted to play the role of criminal, victim, and executioner even as we purportedly learn how to judge, allowing us to experience simultaneously the pleasures and the pains of punishment.

In volume 2, Lovelace enjoys a daydream, a fantasy about what would become of him and his friends if they were to rape Clarissa, Anna Howe, her mother and a maid as they sail to the Isle of Wight. Typically, the rape itself is described as an act of punishment – a punishment, interestingly enough of Mrs Howe's attempt to *judge* him and Clarissa, and of Anna's treatment of him. (How tangled these relationships of punishment and judgment become.) As always, rape is a means of asserting power. He explains: "But why upon her mother, methinks thou askest ... [Because] she believes she acts upon her own judgment; and deserves to be punished for pretending to judgment when she has none. Every living soul, but myself, I can tell thee, shall be punished, that treats either cruelly or disrespectfully so adored a lady. What a plague! Is it not enough that she is teased and tormented in person by me?" (2:419).

Lovelace plays on the notions of punishment and judgment. He will judge his judges for not judging well. He will judge and then he will punish. However, although he has said that "every living soul, but myself ... shall be punished," it is the idea of his *own* punishment (for punishing – i.e. raping) the women which seems to delight him the most. Evidence of this relish might be that while Lovelace's account of the imagined rape takes up little more than a page, his account of his trial goes on for three times that length. It is as if this novel were a kind of machine in which fantasies of punishment were enacted and where those punishments were, in turn, punished themselves. The novel becomes the space in which such fantasies are both encouraged and then controlled, a kind of sado-masochistic dream machine.

This is the way that Lovelace imagines it: "I will suppose ... that all five [of us] are actually brought to trial on this occasion: how bravely shall we enter a court, *I* at the head of you, dressed out each man, as if to his wedding-appearance! You are sure of all the women, old and young, of your side. What brave fellows! What fine gentlemen! There goes a charming handsome man! meaning me, to be sure! Who could find in their hearts to hang such a gentleman as that! whispers one lady ... All will crowd after *me* ... I shall be found to be the greatest criminal; and my safety, for which the general voice will be engaged, will be yours" (2:422). Note the almost inescapable eroticism of his description. The trial is likened to a wedding. Lovelace is thrilled by the idea of thrilling the female spectators, his excitement spurred on by imagining theirs. This is one instance in which Lovelace has no trouble identifying with the female.[18] He identifies with her if she is admiring and desiring *him*. The erotic charge that he gets here seems, furthermore, to be linked to his status as prisoner and thus glamorous victim. Being a victim of this sort appeals to Lovelace because of the attention that it brings.[19]

As in other places in the book, Lovelace's voice is parodic, echoing and grotesquely reflecting Clarissa's situation. Lovelace is making explicit what is covert (though perhaps only slightly so) in the main narrative concerning Clarissa: the ability of another's suffering to move spectators erotically and theatrically. By overtly and even grotesquely theatricalizing the courtroom spectacle, and by an equally overt glamorization of the criminal, Lovelace's speech becomes self-incriminating. Its extreme theatricality serves to distance and distinguish it from the main narrative – Clarissa's own trial and her own beatification.

The scene works as a sort of regulatory check on both text and reader. Since Lovelace is so obviously at fault in what he is doing, the text protects itself from any similar charge. Similarly, the reader of *Clarissa* will seek to distance or distinguish him- or herself from the eroticized, amoral spectators at Lovelace's fantasy trial. These spectators serve as negative examples – models *not* to emulate: "Then, let us look down, look up, look round, which way we will, we shall see all the doors, the shops, the windows, the sign-irons, and balconies (garrets, gutters, and chimney-tops included) all white-capped, black-hooded, and periwigged, or crop-eared up by the *immobile vulgus*: while the floating *street swarmers*, who have seen us pass by at one place, run with stretched-out necks, and strained eyeballs, a round-about way, and elbow and shoulder themselves into places by which we have not passed, in order to obtain another sight of us; every street continuing to pour out its swarm of late-comers, to add to the gathering snowball" (2:423).

Few readers would care to identify themselves with the "stretched-out necks and strained eyeballs" of the "floating street swarmers." An author's note seals our disapproval: "Within these few years past, a passage has been made from the prison to the Sessions-house, whereby malefactors are carried into court without going through the street. Lovelace's triumph on their supposed march shows the wisdom of this alteration" (2:423). Because Lovelace is revelling in display, we know not to trust him. We are therefore, by implication, taught to value Clarissa all the more for her reluctance to display herself. In the parodic scene, elements that were less overt in the main text are brought out: the eroticized nature of criminal-worship and the connections between and among discipline and love, punishment and spectacle.

Another "courtroom" scene takes place in volume 3. In this case the scene is Hampstead, the place to which Clarissa has fled in an attempt to escape Lovelace. Lovelace has found her and has told people that she is simply a shy bride. He has also employed an acquaintance to act as a Captain Tomlinson, an apparent emissary from her family. Three ladies of the house, Widow Bevis, Miss Rawlins, and Mrs Moore, are eager and curious spectators. When Clarissa enters the room, her natural air of authority and integrity cause them to rise as if she were a judge: "But here she comes! cried one, hearing her chamber door open. Here she comes! another, hearing it shut after her – and down dropped the angel among us. We all stood up, bowing and curtsying; and could not help it. For she entered with such an air as commanded all our reverence" (3:107).

What gives Clarissa such a judicial air in this scene is her utter independence, her indifference to anyone else's adulation or approval. Such independence and indifference form the basis of her power. Clarissa demonstrates here the autonomy and self-possession Rousseau valued and which he felt was lost when an actor sought the regard and applause of an audience. It is precisely because Clarissa does not attempt to elicit sympathy that she assumes such power and independence. She says to Lovelace, "Well, well, sir, say what you please. Make me as black as you please. Make yourself as white as you can. I am not now in your power: that consideration will comfort me for all" (3:109). When Captain Tomlinson asks to speak with her privately, she replies, "You may say all that you please to say before these gentlewomen. Mr Lovelace may have secrets. I have none. You seem to think me faulty: I should be glad that all the world knew my heart. Let my enemies sit in judgment upon my actions: fairly scanned, I fear not the result. Let them even ask me my most secret thoughts, and whether they make for or against me, I will reveal them" (3:109).[20] Her independence and indifference here allow her to be uncharacteristically unconcerned with display. For once she is not seeking to slide through her life unnoted. Anyone might look at her through and through, she is saying; she has nothing to hide. This is a kind of artless display which seeks to avoid any hint of the theatricality which so alarmed Rousseau.[21]

Her innocent transparency empowers her. When at one point she nearly catches Tomlinson out in the deception he is enacting, Lovelace explains, "He told me, that just then he thought he felt a sudden flash from her eye, an *eye-beam* as he called it, dart through his shivering reins; and he could not help trembling" (3:112). She similarly turns on Lovelace: "High indignation filled her disdainful eye, eye-beam after eye-beam flashing at me. Every feature of her sweet face had soul in it" (3:116). To judge is to see and to discipline. These "eye-beams" see into the heart of their targets. They see the truth and they punish accordingly. Their effect on Tomlinson is dramatic. Not only does he feel judged and on trial, but he also pleads to Lovelace on Clarissa's behalf: "O sir!, said the captain, as soon as she was gone, what an angel of a woman is this! *I have been*, and I *am*, a very wicked man. But if anything should happen amiss to this admirable lady, through my means, I shall have more cause for self-reproach than for all the bad actions of my life put together. And his eyes glistened" (3:130). Tomlinson had been playing at being a judge of sorts himself, but on receiving Clarissa's all-seeing "eye-beams," he experiences the full force of his own guilt and begs Lovelace to stop his "trial" of Clarissa. Unmanned, his identification with the victimized woman has tempered his previously held maculinity until he is moved to give up his rakish ways.

Tomlinson's emotion at the spectacle of Clarissa's suffering is presented not only as evidence of Clarissa's power, but of his good character as well. *Because* Tomlinson is moved, he himself becomes a good judge. Sympathy leads to good judgment in the sense that Adam Smith intended. With the ability to feel comes the ability to see and to judge.

Tomlinson's response to Clarissa is given predominance in this scene, for he serves as double for both Belford and Lovelace, all of them rakes who have to be taught to feel. The lesson, it seems, is intended for males only. Women, judging from the reaction of the three ladies at Hampstead, feel all too easily, and are thus made fools of: "The women stared. They did nothing but stare" (3:47). And again, "The women stared. (The devil stare ye, thought I! Can ye do nothing but stare?)" (3:48). They are little better than the vulgar street swarmers at Lovelace's imagined trial.

The paradox of sympathy and judgment lies at the heart of this book. In the first scene described above, Lovelace's fantasy trial, the spectators' slavish adoration of the prisoners was presented as vulgar and unconsidered. In this scene, however, the near-conversion of a wicked man by the sight of Clarissa's suffering, his being "moved," carries a far different meaning. Being moved in this way, being capable of this sort of sympathy, seems to be the highest form of judgment. It is this sympathy and this judgment which change Belford forever and give him such authority in the novel. As he writes to Lovelace: "Oh, that thou hadst been there! and in my place! But by what I then felt in myself, I am convinced that a capacity of being moved by the distress of our fellow-creatures is far from being disgraceful to a manly heart" (2:446-7). Belford's "capacity of being moved" ensures his credibility not only as executor of Clarissa's will but also as editor of her papers. Once again, he or she who *feels* the most is the best judge.

This is a paradox, because throughout the novel there are many warnings about the dangers of being "moved" or tricked by "art." Clarissa, after all, is quite literally moved and tricked from her family home by Lovelace. She writes to Anna: "Let this evermore be my caution to individuals of my sex. Guard your eye: 'twill ever be in a combination against your judgment" (2:277), and "the eye is a traitor, and ought ever to be mistrusted" (2:313). If the eye can be deceived, as Clarissa's repeatedly is, on what should people rely? The confusing answer, according to the novel, is sympathy.

The crime of Clarissa's family, for which they are so amply punished at the end of the book, is a failure of sympathy. Clarissa's advice to Anna to distrust the eye is advice her family have followed to their peril. Their distrust is so great that they will not allow themselves to see their daughter for fear that she will move them by means of her "art." Her mother speaks of Clarissa's "power of painting her distresses so as to pierce stone" (4:51), and Mrs Norton advises Clarissa that "your talent at moving the passions is always hinted at" (4:49). The family's hyper-vigilance against being moved becomes, in the end, their downfall. Their own inability to recognize or to sympathize with Clarissa's victimization leads in turn to their own victimization.

Her uncle writes of Clarissa's capacity to move others: "There is no standing against your looks and language," and wonders, "How can you be so unmoved yourself, yet be so able to move everybody else?" (1:304). This question is central. As we have seen, Clarissa never courts the regard of others; she wants, it is said, to slide "through life unnoted."²² Inherent to her virtue is her reluctance to display herself or that virtue. To display virtue would, as we have seen, be to risk or lose it by making it theatrical. The question then becomes, how can we know her virtue if it isn't displayed? How can we be sure that Clarissa is good? This is the very question that drives Lovelace to "try" Clarissa. "What must that virtue be," he asks, "which will not stand a trial" (2:40), and it is the question which fuels the entire narrative. If something cannot be demonstrated by the subject itself, then the subject must be caught, "arrested," objectified, and examined. Clarissa is literally arrested in volume 3, but even before this point she is often described as "entangled" or "ensnared" by the plots of others.²³

Lovelace finds Clarissa to be "impenetrable" and "invincible" (2:36). It is this very indifference and independence which drives him to "try" her. He wants to learn if the unmoved mover can be moved. He is asking, "Is then the divine Clarissa capable of *loving* a man whom she ought *not* to love?" (2:38). He wants to know "Whether her frost be frost indeed" (3:190). He is seeking, in other words, to determine if her virtue might be mere show. If this is the case, as he suspects, then he should be able to surprise from her real sympathy, real love, and real desire.

He is able to trick her into displaying real sympathy and even a sort of love for him when he feigns illness, but the sexual desire he thought to discover he never finds. "She has come out pure gold from the assay," he admits (3:398). As Clarissa herself puts it, "My will is unviolated" (4:186). Her triumph is her refusal to be "moved" out of herself.

The question remains as her uncle asked it, "How can [she] be so unmoved [her]self, yet be so able to move everybody else?" It is this aspect of Clarissa that led me to state in the introduction that the only way to study Clarissa – both the character *and* the text – is to study the responses that she/it generates. There is *no* Clarissa beyond our response to her. There is only the story of how she moves others. She is a magnetic void. This emptiness that attracts is, I suggest, another rewriting of the impossible place (in this case the absolute non-place) of female desire.

Lovelace's trial of Clarissa is an attempt to find that desire. At one point Captain Tomlinson protests that Lovelace is going too far: "You was pleased to tell me, sir, that you only proposed *to try her virtue*" (3:131). But Lovelace is trying her love as well as her virtue. He always thinks that he is at the very point of finding out, or reaching his ever-receding goal of Clarissa's desire: "And as to *trying* her, is she not now in the height of her trial? Have I not reason to think that she is coming about? ... Women often, for their own sakes, will keep the *last secret*." (3:131). It is this "last secret" that Lovelace hopes to trick out of Clarissa: "I love, thou knowest, to trace human nature, and more particularly female nature, through its most secret recesses" (3:139).

Alas, poor Lovelace. That secret he pursues through ever-deeper recesses continues to evade him. There is nothing to see, there is nothing to grasp beyond Clarissa's rejection of him. He succeeds at last in having her, but the victory is hollow. He has to drug her in order to rape her. Because of this, his accomplices, the whores Sally and Polly, taunt him "for leaving the proud lady mistress of her own will, and nothing to *reproach herself with*. And all agreed that the arts used against her on a certain occasion had too high an operation for them or me to judge what her will *would have been* in the arduous trial" (3:276).

In other words, Clarissa escapes from her trial with the mystery of her "will" intact. Even after the rape, the climax of Lovelace's trial of her, the moment which was to have produced the evidence or the truth of her desire, it is *still* impossible to judge what her will would have been. Her desire (at least in the shape that Lovelace might recognize it) is *never* revealed, exposed, or displayed through Lovelace's trial of her.[24]

All that can be known, all that is revealed (and this comes to take the place of the desire that might have been), is her victimization. The place where desire should be or might have been is taken over by pain. Because pain and victimization come to reside in the *place* of desire, or the place near where desire might have been, they come to be seen as woman's desire *itself*. It is because of this substitution and displacement (victimization in the place of desire) that critics such as V.S. Pritchett and others have come to say that Clarissa "wanted" to be raped.

In the introduction, I quoted Jessica Benjamin's question: "How does it come about that femininity appears inextricably linked to passivity, even to masochism, or that women seek their desire in another, hope to have it recognized and recognizable through the subjectivity of an other?" Could we not say that we see the beginnings of an answer in *Clarissa*? Where Lovelace in particular, and the novel in general, sought desire – volition, action, will, agency – we find nothing. In its place is substituted death, pain, violation and martyrdom. The reader is asked to accept Clarissa's martyrdom in place of her desire. The relationship is metonymic. Pain and victimization, repeatedly linked with desire, come eventually to be seen as the heroine's desire in and of themselves.

I opened this chapter by quoting Ian Watt's speculation that novel readers might have something in common with the jurors in a trial. That position, while engaging and difficult, remains safe and distinct from the position of the prisoner on the dock. It seems to me that the reader of *Clarissa* does not enjoy quite such a sanctuary. "It is my design," Belford writes to Lovelace, "to make thee feel" (4:367). That is also the design of the book. The result is a disquieting combination of power and pleasure, innocence and guilt. Clarissa's trial at the hands of Lovelace becomes his own at the hands of Belford. His punishment is to be made to feel what Clarissa might feel. This is sympathy as Adam Smith imagined it – a bridging of the distance between individuals. What Belford wants Lovelace to *feel* through the agency of Clarissa, however, is the effect of his own punishment and trial of her. One man seeks that another feel the punishment he himself inflicted. The route is circular and Clarissa remains the curiously empty and yet compelling vessel through which men feel. She is held so that we can be moved. Our sense of ourselves as subjects and our ability to feel depend upon her.

3 *The Scarlet Letter* and "The Spectacle of the Scaffold"

The phrase, "the spectacle of the scaffold," comes from Foucault (it is the title of one of the chapters in *Discipline and Punish*), but it could serve equally well as a chapter title for Hawthorne's *The Scarlet Letter*. The two books, while very different, share a common obsession: the connections between vision and power. Each can be seen as an investigation of the question, What does looking have to do with punishment? Foucault's demonstration of the pervasive connection in Western culture between vision, power, and punishment is considered one of his great achievements.[1] Hawthorne's novel, published in 1850, engages many of the same issues.

Rereading Hawthorne through the lens of Foucault helps to isolate and focus some of the crucial issues in this novel about punishment and display, but *The Scarlet Letter* brings a term to the discussion that Foucault omits: gender. I would like to investigate the way that *this* mark of difference works among the other economies of discipline, punishment, and visuality in the novel.

The chapter on *Clarissa* showed how the figure of the heroine was in many respects an empty vessel, able to move others while she herself remained arrested or caught. The result was that the subjectivity of Clarissa became defined through her victimization. Her "trial" at the hands of Lovelace revealed or created pain and suffering in the place that desire might have been. Her desire, therefore, could only be represented as masochistic. Hester Prynne is another heroine who takes on the role of martyr, serving as little more than a magnet for our sympathetic attachment.

Both books are concerned with the development of sympathy; both go to great pains to construct the ties which bind us to our heroine. In *Clarissa*, sympathy – tempered with judgment – becomes a means of knowledge, a way to be moved without appearing to succumb to the political and erotic dangers of theatricality. In *The Scarlet Letter* sympathy is more dangerous and more painful, in part, because it is so deeply entwined with guilt.

As readers our identification and sympathy with Hester are routed primarily through Reverend Dimmesdale, her partner in adultery. The novel becomes the story of his deep identification not so much with Hester herself as with her guilt and its emblem, the letter A. For this is an identification not based on a desire to *be* Hester or to suffer as she does (indeed, the argument could be made that Dimmesdale already suffers as much as or more than the heroine), but a desire for the *public mark* of her pain.

In *Discipline and Punish* Foucault tells us that between the middle of the eighteenth and the end of the nineteenth centuries, sweeping changes occurred in the method and style of punishment in Europe. One of the most significant of these was "the disappearance of punishment as spectacle" (8), and "a slackening of the hold on the body" (10). Whereas earlier punishment depended upon prolonged, public physical torture and punishment, the newer, more "humane" methods bypassed the body: "One no longer touched the body, or at least as little as possible, and then only to reach something other than the body itself" (11). That which one tried to reach, though sometimes styled "the heart, the thoughts, the will, the inclinations" was most frequently referred to as the "soul" (16). "At the beginning of the nineteenth century, then, the great spectacle of physical punishment disappeared; the tortured body was avoided; the theatrical representation of pain was excluded from punishment. The age of sobriety had begun" (14). Hawthorne wrote and published his novel in this age of sobriety, but its setting is the earlier age of spectacle. As we will see, this doubled time frame allowed Hawthorne to explore the contradictions and the exclusions of each age. It is in the character of Dimmesdale that these contradictions are played out. Lacking Hester's *public* mark of shame, he is subjected to even greater *private* agonies of the soul.

In one sense Dimmesdale already has a mark of his own (festering on or within his chest), but it is Hester's public display of her mark which both horrifies and attracts him. Unwilling to put himself on display as Hester has been forced to do, Dimmesdale remains repressed and guilty. The sympathy constructed for us in this novel is thus a guilty one. Hawthorne's is a world of repression and guilty secrets, secrets which are held to the breast and only reluctantly revealed. One of those guilty secrets would appear to be a hidden and shameful identification with the female victim.

Such identification has two primary effects. The first is an initial sense of freedom or release. The female victim is held so that the hero and thus we, the readers, can be free. Clarissa is put on trial, arrested so that we might be moved. Hester is kept silent on the scaffold so that Dimmesdale might be free to preach from the pulpit and win praise and fame. Ralph gets a new sense of life and health from watching Isabel choose her fate. Poulet, in "The Phenomenology of Reading," wrote of being energized by the sight of the books on display, being roused to active heroism by the plight of "their immobility." As readers we participate in this energizing process; we too get roused to full subjectivity through the male appreciation of and connection to the female victims. There is, however, a second effect. This is the increasing sense of limitation felt by those characters (male and female alike), a diminution of their powers upon feeling the full impact of the heroine's fate. We are chastened by her pain. *The Scarlet Letter* is notable for the degree to which it is centred almost entirely on the *second* effect. Freedom is imagined, conceived, and constructed only to be almost immediately bound, controlled, and disciplined. Sympathy grants us very little freedom in this novel; instead it acts as a form of discipline. It both attracts and repels, holding us in check.

If *Clarissa* is a study of the heroine as victim in the making, then *The Scarlet Letter* is a study of response to the victim already made. Our gaze is directed away from the heroine herself and onto the mark that signifies her shame and her punishment.[2] It seems to me that this mark carries two messages. The first refers to the wearer; it tells us that she is guilty of a sexual transgression. The mark constructs her as deviant/defiant and thus as a figure of interest. The second message refers not to the wearer, but to the political realm in which she lives. This message informs us that she has met and been judged by authority and power. Much like the seal on an official document or the signature of a dignitary, it is authority's seal branded onto authority's subject. Its message is "the triumph of the law."[3] Thus the dual message of the mark on Hester's breast reminds us both of her deviance/defiance and of the triumph of the law. It marks the conjunction of two realms: the private, the sexual, and the feminine on one hand and the public, the official, and the masculine on the other. Hester is marked as female and as criminal. This doubled identity makes her a powerful and troubling figure. The mark she wears on her breast proclaims not just the exposure and punishment of her deviance and defiance, but their very possibility. Such a conjunction, or indeed collision, of meanings grants the symbol a seemingly magnetic power over those who encounter it.

To explore the operation of this power, I turn to a scene at the end of the novel, in chapter 22, in which Hester Prynne stands amid a holiday crowd. In some respects, this scene is reminiscent of Lovelace's imagined trial scene in *Clarissa*, when he saw himself as the centre of attention at a public trial, much like Hester. But he imagined that event as a thrilling spectacle, filled with movement, tension, and excitement. Here a kind of stasis is imposed upon the scene; spectators and spectacle alike are held frozen in their places. There is tension, but no movement. The excitement, if there is any, transfixes rather than enlivens.

Although the narrator tells us that her own townspeople had become accustomed to the letter she wore upon her breast, visitors had never seen anything like it: "These, after exhausting other modes of amusement, now thronged about Hester Prynne with rude and boorish intrusiveness. Unscrupulous as it was, however, it could not bring them nearer than a circuit of several yards. At that distance they accordingly stood, fixed there by the centrifugal force of the repugnance which the mystic symbol inspired" (166). Something about the symbol exerts a powerful force. The "unscrupulous ... boorish intrusiveness" which impels the crowd to surround Hester is physically checked by a counter-motion, "repugnance," a force which keeps spectators at a prescribed distance. There are twin forces at work – that which attracts and that which repels – which seem to "fix" *both* spectators and spectacle. Clarissa, unable to move herself, was at least able to move others. Here, spectator and spectacle alike are held and arrested by the symbol Hester must wear.

That Hester should be "fixed" by the mark on her breast is perhaps to be expected. We saw how Clarissa was repeatedly described as ensnared, arrested, and held. What is surprising is the degree to which the "A" controls the spectators as well. The letter seems to exert a kind of magnetic repulsion, a negative sympathy which pushes people away: "As was usually the case wherever Hester stood, a small, vacant area – a sort of magic circle – had formed itself about her, into which though the people were elbowing one another at a little distance, none ventured, or felt disposed to intrude. It was a forcible type of the moral solitude in which the scarlet letter enveloped its fated wearer" (158). The A, symbol of woman's deviance and the law's triumph, encloses Hester in solitude. It arrests and immobilizes not only the wearer, but also those she encounters.

Something of the same sort of dance of attraction and repulsion is enacted in "The Custom House." There, the narrator, recounting his first discovery of the scarlet letter in an attic, comments on its fascination for him. He describes it as "the object that most drew my attention" (24), and continues: "It strangely interested me. My eyes fastened themselves upon the old scarlet letter, and would not be turned aside. Certainly there was some deep meaning in it, most worthy of interpretation, and which, as it were, streamed forth from the mystic symbol, subtly commmunicating itself to my sensibilities, but evading the analysis of my mind" (25). He dwells on the mysteriously magnetic properties of the faded piece of cloth, registered by a sense other than intellect. A meaning too subtle for the mind to grasp "stream[s] forth" and calls him.

It appears, however, that to respond to this call can be dangerous. The narrator places the letter on his own breast, and is scorched: "It seemed to me, then, that I experienced a sensation not altogether physical, yet almost so, as of burning heat; and as if the letter were not of red cloth, but red-hot iron. I shuddered and involuntarily let it fall upon the floor" (25). Like the spectators in chapter 22, he is drawn toward the letter only to be almost physically pushed back. The mark of guilt and suffering has the power to reach and affect us over centuries, beyond and through fiction.

By trying to wear the scarlet letter himself, the narrator of "The Custom House" seems to be both describing and enacting the process of identification in *The Scarlet Letter*. Both his desire to put the scarlet letter on and the pain it causes him prefigure Dimmesdale's cross-gender identification. Such desire and pain also figure centrally in the reader's response. Our identification is built from the same elements: attraction and repulsion, desire and pain.

These scenes – the one, narrated in an intimate way by the author, the story of his own "identification," and the other, from a more distant narratorial perspective describing the public's encounter with the letter – serve as two accounts of the process of identification in this novel, two models of the process to be undertaken by the reader. The narrator's interaction with the letter is immediate and direct. He feels irresistibly drawn toward the faded A, picks it up, places it on his chest, gets burned, and drops it. The scene in chapter 22, while retaining the same dynamic of attraction and repulsion, is structured differently. In the first place, that scene is public rather than private. Furthermore, in contrast to the narrator of "The Custom House," who encounters only the symbol of the crime, the spectators are faced with a real woman.

Our own identification in the novel is also built out of two conflicting forces, our guilty *identification* with the spectators who surround her and our sense of our own *difference* from (and superiority toward) them. They serve as foils, as models we should *not* emulate. What they are doing is portrayed as both uncivilized (they are sailors with "sunburnt and desperado-looking faces") and barbaric or even inhuman (they are Indians with "snake-like black eyes") (166). These spectators, unlike us, are encountering Hester and the letter for the first time. Their very "strangeness" is underscored. They are unfamiliar with Hester and her mark. They appear at the end of the novel when the readers, like Hester's own townspeople, may have become inured to the symbol and its punishing effects and may have developed sympathy for its wearer. The newcomers' reaction, therefore, serves all the more as a contrast to our own. We join the narrator in his condemnation of their activity because we, like him, are privy to her feelings and thoughts. We learn, for example, that their scrutiny "tormented" Hester (167), "subject[ing] [her] to another trial" (166). Our own place is constructed by showing our similarity with, *and* difference from the spectators. *Like* them, we are drawn forward and then repelled. *Unlike* them, we are granted some knowledge of what Hester is feeling, for we have encountered her before. (This knowledge makes us judges of her judges, critics of her critics.) We judge the spectators on the evidence we are given of Hester's emotional state (knowledge they cannot share). Our evidence is that "the burning letter ... was thus made to sear her breast more painfully than at any time since the first day she put it on" (167).

These spectators, presented as persecutors and judges, re-enact the scene at the beginning of the novel in which part of Hester's punishment is to stand on the scaffold and face her community. Hester, facing the newcomers, must re-enact that moment of shame and exposure. Display becomes, once again, a form of punishment. The process shows us how curiosity (in this case that of the strangers), which to a large extent mirrors our own as readers, however innocent in intent, can be savage and can hurt. The knowledge of Hester's pain increases our sympathy, but it is a sympathy based on guilt because we recognize our identification with the spectators and seek to differentiate ourselves from them. This sympathy is a reaction against the spectators' overt, and our own covert, savage curiosity, and is used as a force to neutralize or override punishing judgment. Constructed in equal measure out of identification with those who stare fixedly at the mystic symbol and a sense of our own difference from them, our sympathy is guilty from the start.

Traditionally, sympathy has been viewed as an antidote to judgment, a means of nullifying its cruel effects. It is represented as all that a viewer, author, or reader can offer a heroine/victim. But if sympathy can only come *after* judgment, if it *depends* upon pain and suffering for its existence, then the relationship between punishment and sympathy is neither so simple nor so innocent as it might seem.[4] There is a deeper attachment to scenes of punishment, guilt, and pain than the sentimental and traditional view of sympathy will admit. Richard Brodhead has noted: "*The Scarlet Letter* is known as the great novel of seventeenth-century Puritanism. But ... the striking fact about *The Scarlet Letter* is that it is almost exclusively the Puritan disciplinary system – its prison house, stocks, scaffold, and penal letters, not its practice of piety or its habit of trade – that Hawthorne concerns himself with"(77) Brodhead's implication is that Hawthorne's obsession with discipline and punishment has been overlooked – or misread. Much has been written about Hawthorne's interest in the concept of sympathy,[5] but his use of sympathy and discipline as forces which counteract and compensate for each other has not been explored.

Thinking of our sympathy as a contrast to the "boorish" and "unscrupulous" curiosity of the spectators in Chapter 22 is the conventional approach.[6] We think of ourselves as superior to them, more enlightened. Often associated with this sense of superiority and enlightenment is a further sense of liberation and freedom, but the sympathy we are taught in *The Scarlet Letter* does not so much liberate as bind and pain. This novel, like all the others considered in this book, can be viewed as a "school of sympathy." Unlike the others, however, the lesson in sympathy offered in this novel becomes a lesson in discipline, restraint, and pain as well.

That lesson is begun in "The Custom-House." Here Hawthorne begins to construct his reader by beginning the lessons on sympathy and restraint. At first his view seems to be expansive: "When he casts his leaves forth upon the wind, the author addresses, not the many who will fling aside his volume, or never take it up, but the few who will understand him, better than most of his schoolmates and lifemates" (4). This, so far, is perfectly clear. We are flattered to hear that we belong to a small but select group ("the few who will understand him"), and we are no doubt pleased to dissociate ourselves from the non-discriminating multitude. That which follows, however, is less straightforward and less reassuring:

Some authors, indeed, do far more than this, and indulge themselves in such confidential depths of revelation as could fittingly be addressed, only and exclusively, to the one heart and mind of perfect sympathy; as if the printed book, thrown at large on the wide world, were certain to find out the divided segment of the writer's own nature, and complete his circle of existence by bringing him into communion with it. It is scarcely decorous, however, to speak all, even where we speak impersonally. But – as thoughts are frozen and utterance benumbed, unless the speaker stand in some true relation with his audience – it may be pardonable to imagine that a friend, a kind and apprehensive, though not the closest friend, is listening to our talk; and then, a native reserve being thawed by this genial consciousness, we may prate of the circumstances that lie around us, and even of ourself, but still keep the inmost Me behind its veil. To this extent and within these limits, an author, methinks, may be autobiographical, without violating either the reader's rights or his own. (4-5)

I have quoted this passage at length to give its dilatory and evasive flavour in full. Its winding circumlocutions are difficult to trace
because each time a position seems to be taken, it is almost as
quickly reversed. Hawthorne initially sketches a portrait of a ful-
filling relationship between author and reader only to claim that *he*
will not be like those authors who say too much. That, after all,
would be "scarcely decorous." While it may be "pardonable," he
claims, to view the reader as a friend, he is careful to limit the relationship by stating, "Not the closest friend." Coyly he protests that
he wants to "keep the inmost Me behind its veil." Only "to this
extent and within these limits," he claims, can his enterprise be
acceptable.

Each time, a possibility is created, whether it be finding "the one
heart and mind of perfect sympathy," completing "the circle of his
existence," or addressing his "closest friend," that possibility is as
quickly discounted. Hawthorne sets a "limit" on it or dismisses it
altogether. The specter of perfect sympathy is raised and then
snatched away. Desire is expressed and then reined in. Each time, a
stern hand of control is placed on the relationship between author
and reader. Decorum and the law are partners in the establishment
of limits, the transgression of which would be a violation of "the
reader's rights or his own."[7]

The effect of such evasion and control is not, however, entirely
negative. The repression or the banishment of that which is "scarcely decorous," and that which may *not* "be pardonable" is incomplete. The effect instead is the creation of a kind of productive confusion. By describing what *might* be and then dismissing it, Hawthorne ensures that the ghost of that presence is evoked, lingers,
and never disappears. An author is imagined who "indulges" in
"confidential depths of revelation," only to be dismissed. The perfect reader is called forward and then instructed to keep at a distance. This invocation and subsequent negation, assertion followed
by denial, becomes one of the distinguishing moves in *The Scarlet
Letter*. By describing the kind of relationship author and reader are
not going to have, Hawthorne merely banishes that relationship to
a kind of spectral limbo, a sphere from which it can and will return.
This is surprising because Hawthorne, of all authors, should know
that ghosts haunt, and that the repressed returns.

Perhaps the reason that sympathy has to be rigidly controlled is
that its very existence is so important to Hawthorne. This is an anx-

iety that he seems to have shared with Adam Smith. As David Marshall writes of Smith, "The theater of sympathy in *The Theory of Moral Sentiments* is based on the simultaneous necessity of spectators and fear of spectators; the ultimate threat in the world that Smith represents is the prospect of spectators who would deny sympathy" (*Figure of Theater* 191).

"Spectators who would deny sympathy": many passages in *The Scarlet Letter* can be read as dramatizations of this fear. At both the beginning and the end of the novel, for example, Hester is surrounded by unsympathetic crowds. The narrator's comment on the crowd awaiting Hester's release outside the prison door is that "Meagre, indeed, and cold, was the sympathy that a transgressor might look for, from such bystanders at the scaffold" (37). The narrator in "The Custom House" who decides to "keep the inmost Me behind its veil" seems to be worried about a similar sort of exposure. In both cases the fear and anxiety echo Smith's: "According to Smith, the exposure we fear ... is exposure before the eyes of those who can not or will not enter into our suffering, imagine our place and point of view – at the moment we are most in need of sympathy. (Marshall, *The Figure of Theater* 185). This situation, a lone figure facing a crowd, hoping for sympathy and almost certain not to find it, is that of both Hester on the scaffold and the author, Hawthorne, with his novel. Both are putting themselves on display; both hope for an understanding response.

We can be fairly certain that Hawthorne both read and was influenced by Smith's *Theory of Moral Sentiments*.[8] His vision of sympathy certainly seems similar in many respects. Of Hester's first sojourn on the scaffold he writes: "There can be no outrage, methinks, against our common nature ... more flagrant than to forbid the culprit to hide his face for shame" (41). "It was," he continues, "almost intolerable to be borne" (42). He describes her walk to the scaffold in this way: "Haughty as her demeanor was, she perchance underwent an agony from every footstep of those that thronged to see her, as if her heart had been flung into the street for them all to spurn and trample upon" (40). The fact that Hester is a woman surely intensifies our sense of agony, that that which is considered private and domestic, the young mother with her newborn, should be exposed to the public view.

When Lovelace imagined his own walk from jail to courtroom, he saw it as a sort of triumphant procession or wedding march with himself as a hero to adoring female fans. Hawthorne imagines it differently. He dwells on the horror of having to be exposed to the public eye. This would be a horror that Clarissa Harlowe shared, but Clarissa never lived long enough to have to experience what it might mean to be continually in the public eye. *The Scarlet Letter*, by contrast, is an extended study of life lived after the mark of punishment and shame has been imposed. We were told that to be "the subject of public talk" must "hurt" Clarissa. A defining feature of her virtue was her desire to "slide through life unnoted." If to be the subject of public talk must hurt, then *The Scarlet Letter* is an examination of just how much, and in what ways, that hurt hurts.

While the threat of exposure in Hawthorne's novel is certainly terrifying and pervasive (signaled by its images of "intolerable" suffering and "trampled hearts"), there remains, nonetheless, a giddy sense of thrill in exposure – even a secret longing to be seen. How else could one take the stage in Puritan New England? How else could one get such riveted attention from the crowd? Even a preacher might not expect quite such an attentive audience. The desire to be seen and noticed would still, in Hawthorne's nineteenth-century Massachusetts, carry something of the same stigma it carried for the Puritans.[9]

Foucault described the nineteenth century as the "age of sobriety in punishment." Writing from within that era, Hawthorne is looking back to a time that was both more repressive and more spectacular than his own. One can no longer perform or conduct "the spectacle of the scaffold" in public. The work of punishment must instead be played out privately, within one's own breast.

It was the expression of just such a desire to be seen and admired that made Lovelace's fantasy of becoming a criminal-hero so scandalous. In *Clarissa* such a desire could be openly expressed by Lovelace and censured in the text, but in *The Scarlet Letter* the desire is never given voice directly. Instead, it is a longing that that can only be "heard" or "read" in the evasions, negations and denials of the text. The reader's ear must be sympathetically tuned in order to catch it. The epistolary style of *Clarissa* makes eavesdroppers or voyeurs of all its readers. The revelation of secrets in *The Scarlet Letter*, on the other hand, must be more carefully and artfully arranged. To speak too openly would be to reveal too much. Only when our hearts are properly attuned are we allowed to look, or even *able* to see. It is sympathy which allows us to see and to hear.

In both novels the desire to appear as a spectacle, particularly as a spectacle of punishment, involves a kind of cross-gender identification. By imagining himself as hero/victim, Lovelace seeks for himself a place similar to that which Clarissa enjoys in the novel – star attraction, star victim. Dimmesdale's longing to show himself is coded along the same lines. He also wants to be in Hester's place. In each case a male author presents a female heroine who is pushed into the limelight against her will. In each case, in order for male characters (Lovelace and Dimmesdale) to imagine themselves as similarly beheld, they have to imagine themselves as female. To identify with the female is to identify with the victim. To identify with the victim is to identify with the one on display, the spectacle.[10] Female, victim, spectacle: the terms merge until they are nearly indistinguishable.

It is perhaps the entangled nature of these prohibitions and desires that makes the expression of the desire to be seen so complicated, and practically unspeakable. One can only approach it, can only arrange to be displayed, cautiously and circuitously. In a letter to his wife before their marriage, Hawthorne wrote: "I am glad to think that God sees through my heart ... and so may any mortal, who is capable of full sympathy and therefore worthy to come into my depths. But he must find his own way there."[11] Like Adam Smith, Hawthorne expresses concern about being exposed to one who might withhold sympathy. Only someone capable of *full* sympathy is worthy to come into Hawthorne's depths. That person must find his or her own way; the author will not help by providing a display. This is the type of sympathy the novel attempts to teach its readers: to become "worthy" enough to find our way into the depth's of Hawthorne's novel and Hawthorne's heart. Sympathy provides us a way to see and to be seen, but in Hawthorne's world, it must be carefully regulated. Read in this way, the novel becomes little more than the construction of a safe environment for display – a place where guilty secrets and "inmost Me[s]" can be revealed but not reviled. The female, displayed against her will, is the vehicle through which the male may enjoy the same fantasy.

Gordon Hutner, who provides this reference to Hawthorne's letter, sees in it a "call for a special intuition" (or sympathy) on the part of both wife and ideal reader that is particularly Romantic. He explains: "For Hawthorne, sympathy imparts a Romantic ideal of communication; it predicates an understanding that passes beyond words" (8). While the influence of Romanticism on Hawthorne is undeniable,[12] we have to be more specific. With what eye, after all, are we seeing in *The Scarlet Letter*? Does our own gaze not encompass *both* the gaze of the Puritans of Massachusetts *and* the gaze of the nineteenth-century narrator? Hawthorne certainly employs Romantic concepts of sympathy, but he always does so in counterpoint – setting them off against earlier and sometimes contradictory notions. Why is *The Scarlet Letter* set two hundred years prior to its time of writing if not to exploit the double vision such retrospection provides?

Hawthorne mixes seventeenth-, eighteenth- and nineteenth-century uses of the term sympathy to interesting effect. But before examining this blending in particular, it might be beneficial to give a swift overview of Hawthorne's use of retrospection in general.

Clarissa is renowned for the immediacy of its epistolary style, its "writing to the moment." *The Scarlet Letter* by contrast always looks to the past, to what has already occurred. This is true in several senses. First, the "crime" committed by Hester and Dimmesdale is well over by the time the story begins. Furthermore Hester, unlike her sister heroine, Clarissa, has already been judged and her punishment begun before the book opens. This sense of events being "over," finished, in the past and yet still spilling into the present, has come to be seen as something of a hallmark of Hawthorne's fiction. The past is always *in* Hawthorne's present, or at the very least, is never far behind.

The most obvious use of retrospection in *The Scarlet Letter* is its seventeenth-century setting. The span of two hundred years between the doing and the telling allows Hawthorne to create what I call a "stereo-scopic" gaze, a way of looking in two directions at once. What this means is that he can adopt either a pre-enlightenment perspective (typical of the Puritan community he portrays) or a post-enlightenment "modern" perspective, which sees some elements of that society as barbarous or inhumane.[13] The narration alternates between a seventeenth-century mode of seeing and a seemingly more "natural" nineteenth-century mode. Each viewpoint unsettles, undercuts, and de-naturalizes the other.

By maintaining *both* perspectives, by alternating from one to another, Hawthorne provides himself with the means of "having it both ways." He can be condescending and derisive about the ways of his forefathers and never lose his own obsession with those ways. He can censure and judge the events of Puritan Massachusetts while at the same time maintaining the ability to experience them through fiction. In *Clarissa* we could play the roles of victim *and* executioner, could experience the life of both prisoner *and* judge. Hawthorne's double vision allows us the same latitude. We can join the "rude and boorish" throng which surrounds Hester in chapter 22, and we can judge them from afar.

Hawthorne's double gaze also allows him to incorporate two distinctive views of punishment. Foucault tells us that somewhere between the beginning of the eighteenth century and the end of the nineteenth, "the entire economy of punishment was redistributed"(*Discipline* 7). Public executions disappeared, marking "both the decline of the spectacle" and "a slackening hold on the body" (10). One no longer touched the body, or at least as little as possible, and then only to reach something other than the body itself" (11). What was it that was sought. The answer says Foucault "is simple, almost obvious ... it must be the soul" (16). Hawthorne's stereo-scopic gaze allows him to utilize the tension in the contradiction between these two methods of punishment in order to create his own spectacle. Dimmesdale's drama centres around his double anguish, the pain of both soul and body (his putative festering sore on his chest). Hawthorne is thus able to create a new nineteenth-century spectacle, one that reaches for the soul without abandoning or "slackening" its hold on the body.

The play of one time period against the other serves as another form of discipline, a discipline that acts, however, as a productive force. This is the by-now-familiar strategy of invocation and denial. When, for example, a light appears in the sky, the narrator half-earnestly and half-scornfully reports that "nothing was more common, in those days, than to interpret all meteoric appearances, and other natural phenomena ... as so many revelations from a supernatural source" (106). The earlier science is half mocked, but never entirely discredited. It is allowed to remain so as to add a note of mystery and darkness to the "modern" commonsensical view of natural phenomena. The effect of allowing the two views to rest side by side, neither wholly submitting to the other, is that neither is obliterated and neither is triumphant. Each is disciplined (that is, reined in and controlled) by the other. The result is the same sort of productive confusion that we saw in Hawthorne's construction of the reader in his introduction. Powerful images and powerful emotions are evoked only to be denied or repressed. A suggestion is made only to be withdrawn. To assert and to contradict like this is to allow oneself license to say the unsayable.[14]

Hawthorne uses the same ambivalence and double vision in his construction of sympathy. By the mid-nineteenth century, when Hawthorne was writing *The Scarlet Letter*, the term had gone through a number of varied and sometimes contradictory meanings. Hawthorne calls on and uses several of these, some contemporary, and others anachronistic. James Rodgers explains the use of the term during the eighteenth century: "The three main uses of sympathy ... were as: (1) an occult force, spurned by mechanistic science; (2) a useful physiological concept, revived by the mechanists amd taken over by their opponents; and (3) a social mechanism or sentiment important to moral philosophy". (134). The first of these usages, the basis of alchemy, would be used to explain how two apparently different substances seek each other out. The second concept concerned the nature of the relationship between various organs of the body and even between body and soul or body and spirit. The third usage was that expounded by Adam Smith in his *Theory of Moral Sentiments* (1759) in which sympathy is posited as a type of moral "glue" which can bind a society of isolated individuals together.[15] Hawthorne employed all these concepts in *The Scarlet Letter*.

For Hawthorne the nineteenth-century meaning of sympathy, while still retaining some of its previous connotations, took on a decidedly Romantic cast. Thus, while retaining its social sense as an agency which could transcend individuals' isolation and help bind them together, sympathy began to be seen as primarily an aesthetic force.[16] In other words, poetry and art, or more precisely the vision of the *poet* or *artist*, were considered to be the primary means of exerting and experiencing sympathy. Sympathy came to mean a projective identification, a method of achieving imaginary or artistic union. M.H. Abrams explains that Coleridge used the eighteenth-century notion of the term "to explain how a poet is able to annul space ... and become ... the personality he [sic] contemplates" (245). It is this Romantic sense of the word sympathy which Hawthorne seems to be conjuring when he says that only a mortal "capable of full sympathy" is "worthy to come into my depths." The reader, it seems, must have the gifts of a great poet to be able to merge with the author and read correctly.[17] This Romantic concept of sympathy is central to an understanding of *The Scarlet Letter*.

However, by setting his novel in the seventeenth century, Hawthorne gave himself license to work with the earlier meanings and connotations of sympathy as well. Just as in "The Custom House" he constructed his reader by evoking and then denying a possiblity of sympathetic communion, so he similarly plays the two uses of sympathy off against each other in the main narrative. The result, as in the custom house passage, is a productive confusion. Through the use of what I call his stereo-scopic vision, allowing him to see two ways at once, Hawthorne was able to employ early and contemporary meanings of sympathy in such a way that the meanings intertwine, enrich and subvert each other.[18]

It is in the portrait of Chillingworth that the seventeenth- and eighteenth-century scientific uses of sympathy are primarily exploited. Early in the novel, Chillingworth says that he will use the same alchemical methods which he had used in the old country to seek Hester's adulterous partner in the new, and will employ the same principle of sympathy: "I shall seek this man, as I have sought truth in books; as I have sought gold in alchemy. There is a sympathy that will make me conscious of him" (54). Sympathy is to be used as a tool to reveal and subject the other.

Hawthorne's stereo-scopic vision allows him to discredit Chillingworth in two ways simultaneously. The first is by identifying him with the pseudo-science of alchemy and thereby implying that his science is out of date, mere hocus-pocus or black magic.[19] The second reference is more contemporary. These portrayals of Chillingworth expose the dangers or discomforts of what we now recognize as modern-day police or psychiatric surveillance. What is chilling about Chillingworth is his diabolic thoroughness and efficiency, his ability to see right to the centre of his prey. In Chillingworth are united the "black arts" of pre-enlightenment magic and the supervisory and disciplining gaze of Jeremy Bentham's panopticon. What is so effective and so frightening about the panopticon and the disciplinary society which it embodies, according to Foucault, is the way that while remaining invisible itself, "it imposes on those whom it subjects a principle of compulsory visibility" (*Disci-*

pline and Punish, 187). Chillingworth imposes just such a state on Dimmesdale.

Chillingworth's deployment of sympathy is described thus: "Few secrets can escape an investigator, who has opportunity and license to undertake such a quest, and skill to follow it up. A man burdened with a secret should especially avoid the intimacy of his physician. If the latter possess native sagacity, and ... intuition; if he show no intrusive egotism ... if he have the power ... to bring his mind into such affinity with his patient's ... then, at some inevitable moment, will the soul of the sufferer be dissolved ... bringing all its mysteries into the daylight" (86). There is no chance of keeping the "inmost Me behind a veil" from a man, from a gaze, like this one. What is especially pernicious is the physician's "native sagacity," his "intuition," and his ability "to bring his mind into ... affinity with his patient's."

The ability to think and feel like his patient, to (in Henry James' phrase) "get into the skin of" the other,[20] is perhaps what Stephen Greenblatt had in mind when he claimed that empathy could be used as a tool for exploitation or colonization. Empathy, he writes, implies "the ruthless displacement and absorption of the other" (236). This is what scares Dimmesdale so about his "friend." It is Chillingworth's capacity for sympathy that makes him so dangerous. His is a sympathy that is used like a spotlight or a police searchlight to reveal and to destroy.[21] It has been noted that Chillingworth serves here as a prototype of the modern psychiatrist.[22] He is also, I would suggest, a prototype of the modern police detective. It is the dark, intrusive, and sadistic underside of sympathy which is being explored here.

Such intrusive burrowings prompt Dimmesdale, when he learns of Chillingworth's true identity, to exclaim, "O Hester Prynne, thou little, little knowest all the horror of this thing! And the shame! – the indelicacy! – the horrible ugliness of this exposure of a sick and guilty heart to the very eye that would gloat over it!" (132). Such an exclamation rings with the familiar tones of Adam Smith, who saw in sympathy a type of shield against just such exposure.[23] Hester tries to assure Dimmesdale that he can *escape* Chillingworth's punishing gaze: "Is there not shade enough in all this boundless forest to hide thy heart from the gaze of Roger Chillingworth?" she asks (134). Foucault would answer Hester's question in the negative. "Disciplinary power," he writes, "is everywhere and always alert, since by its very principle it *leaves no zone of shade*" (*Discipline and Punish*, 177, emphasis my own). The text would seem to agree; there is no escape. The characters must continue to exist, at the very least, in the glare and the gaze of the novel and its readers.

The sympathy Chillingworth deploys is represented for us, the readers, so that we might both use it and despise it. We use it because we need it in order to see with Chillingworth into the guilty heart of Dimmesdale. We use it, but are also instructed to hate and reject it. As in several other cases noted above, readers are presented with characters whose responses we are to emulate as well as characters whose responses we are meant to reject.[24]

What is particularly significant about the Chillingworth-Dimmesdale relationship is its centrality in the novel. I mentioned in the introduction that in all four novels discussed in the main body of this study, the story of the bonds between the men surrounding the heroine threatens to become the central narrative, eclipsing our view of her. Nowhere is this more true than in *The Scarlet Letter*. Dimmesdale is in many respects more suffering heroine than Hester Prynne herself.

The novel does attempt to envision or create another less sinister type of sympathy than that practiced by Chillingworth, one which would allow knowledge of others without any violation of their "rights." It is questionable, however, whether this sympathy ultimately produces effects any more liberating or positive than those created by Chillingworth, or whether it merely serves to implicate the sympathiser in the same position of pain as he or she who suffers.

The "real" or "good" sympathy in *The Scarlet Letter* is almost always portrayed as a nonvisual and nonrational experience: "When an uninstructed multitude attempts to see with its eyes, it is exceedingly apt to be deceived. When, however, it forms its judgment, as it usually does, on the intuitions of its great and warm heart, the conclusions thus attained are often so unerring, as to possess the character of truths supernaturally revealed" (88). Chillingworth is the only active looker in this novel and his cold scientific gaze is repeatedly censured by the text. There seems to be something about visual observation that, for Hawthorne, disrupts or obviates the occurrence of real sympathy. Instead he accords primacy to the aural. That which enters the ear seems to be somehow purer, to have a better chance of bypassing the eyes and mind and reaching the heart directly.

Part of the reason the aural seems to succeed is that it transcends both the intellect and, ironically, language itself.[25] This is particularly evident in the effect of Dimmesdale's sermons: "The young pastor's voice was tremulously sweet, rich, deep, and broken. The feeling that it so evidently manifested, rather than the direct purport of the words, caused it to vibrate within all hearts, and brought the listeners into one accord of sympathy" (49). It is the *feeling*, not the meaning of the words, which brings the listeners into sympathy. Their response is below or beyond reason: "The people knew not the power that moved them thus" (98).

In his last sermon, only Hester can detect the actual reason for, or source of, the minister's passion. (Here sympathy is being routed through the female for the male – yet another role reversal in a novel which is full of them.) Once again, the meaning is beyond anything that language can express: "Hester Prynne listened with such intentness, and sympathized so intimately, that the sermon had throughout a meaning for her, entirely apart from its indistinguishable words" (164). Hester, standing outside the church, does not know what the minister is saying inside, but it does not matter. Because she has sympathetic knowledge of his guilt, she is able to hear what it is that he is saying without distinguishing a single word. The passion of his suffering is so great that others, even if they do not know the explicit source of his anguish, can also begin to detect it: "Still, if the auditor listened intently, and for the purpose, he could detect the same cry of pain" (165). That cry is described as a "loud or low expression of anguish, – the whisper, or the shriek ... of suffering humanity, that touched a sensibility in every bosom" (164).[26] True or "full" sympathy, it appears, must not or cannot be represented either visually or through language. Sympathy, in these passages, operates as if by magic. In this sense, it retains some of its pre-nineteenth-century associations with alchemy and with a mystery at once scientific and nonrational.[27] It operates as an unseen force that can be best apprehended through the suspension of vision and of language. Furthermore, it can only be caught or "heard" by someone able to sympathize with guilt.

The sympathy for which the minister's speech asks is readily accorded because it requires no effort. It is a kind of spontaneous "elective affinity." Granted automatically, with no effort or will on the part of the sympathizer, it responds to guilt. Only the guilty, like Hester, can properly hear the underlying message of Dimmesdale's sermon, the "cry of pain" which lurks beneath his prophecy of a great future for the republic.

We can get an idea of how such a transaction of guilty sympathy or sympathetic guilt might work by what we learn of Hester's situation. Her sense of her own guilt heightens her awareness of the guilt of others: "It now and then appeared to Hester ... that the scarlet letter had endowed her with a new sense. She shuddered to believe, yet could not help believing that it gave her a sympathetic knowledge of the hidden sin in other hearts" (61). Once guilty, like young Goodman Brown, one sees guilt everywhere. This recognition serves to both connect and to separate: the scarlet letter "had such potent and disastrous efficacy that no human sympathy could reach her, save it were sinful like herself" (62).

Thus, the reader is involved in a kind of moral catch-22: "No human sympathy could reach her save it were sinful like herself." Any reader who wants to move into a closer relationship with Hester is, as it were, stopped at the gate. This is a club for sinners only. To sympathize with Hester is to acknowledge one's own guilt. Only by acknowledging our guilt can we sympathize.

Pearl, like her mother, is often presented as being in a sphere by herself, as being isolated from the rest of society. The sympathy which the text, the reader, and the author are expected to extend to Hester, Pearl is expected to produce for herself: "She [Pearl] wanted – what some people want through life – a grief that should deeply touch her, and thus humanize and make her capable of sympathy" (126). This statement would seem to imply that grief is what "humanizes" us, is the catalyst that allows to feel the proper kind of sympathy. This sympathy, unlike the utilitarian sympathy practised by Chillingworth which objectifies and separates, actually draws people together and unites them through their pain.

In *Clarissa* only Lovelace ever dared to make a similar wish. He occasionally expressed the hope that Clarissa would feel pain, so that she might come down from her lofty sphere and exist on his plane. In that novel his assertion that Clarissa might "need" or "want" a little pain was presented as a cruel and sadistic wish. (His rape can be read as the manifestation of this wish.) Here the wish is overt: "She wanted ... a grief," and it is granted: "Pearl kissed his lips. A spell was broken. The great scene of grief, in which the wild infant bore a part, had developed all her sympathies" (173). Pearl is amply rewarded for her induction into the world of grief and pain. She inherits a fortune, moves to Europe, and marries royalty.

Just as Pearl has to feel pain before she can experience sympathy and be human, so we, the readers, have to feel pain and acknowledge our own guilt in order to know and apprehend the characters' suffering. When Hester first appears, in chapter 2, the narrator comments that "there was something exquisitely painful in it" (39). The proximity of the words "exquisite" and "painful" produces a disquieting effect, as if by learning to appreciate the aesthetics of suffering, one could become a connoisseur of pain. Sympathy may only be gained through guilt, but there appear to be some aesthetic rewards.

The character of Hester has puzzled generations of readers. She seems in many ways to be the embodiment of bold and passionate womanhood. What, then, are we to make of the ending of the novel in which Hester voluntarily returns to the colony in order to resume her life of submission and penance: "She had returned, therefore, and resumed, – of her own free will, for not the sternest magistrate of that iron period would have imposed it" (177). She takes up the letter again, this time for good. Once, earlier on in the forest, she had flung her letter and her cap aside in the name of freedom, only to be forced to reluctantly put them back on. There she had done it with "a sense of inevitable doom upon her" (143), and we were told that "Hester next gathered up the heavy tresses of her hair, and confined them beneath her cap. As if there were a withering spell in the sad letter, her beauty, the warmth and richness of her womanhood, departed, like fading sunshine; and a gray shadow seemed to fall across her" (143).

Why would an act that spelled "doom" and the sacrifice of warmth and beauty in the middle of the novel become, by the end, an act of heroism? Sacvan Bercovitch sees The Scarlet Letter as itself performing the same function as the letter and the cap in the forest scene. All work "to rein in," to control and to discipline. He writes that, like the letter and the cap, Hawthorne's novel functions precisely to rein in what "becomes possible" ("A-Morality" 19).

Bercovitch continues by musing on the statement in the middle of the novel that "the scarlet letter had not done its office," that Hester was not yet sufficiently inwardly chastened: "The scarlet letter had not done 'its office': the entire novel asks us to interpret this in the affirmative, and by the end *compels* us to, as a grim necessity. It is as though Hawthorne had to overcompensate for the enormous radical potential inherent in his characters and symbols; had to find some moral absolute ... powerful enough to recall all those unleashed energies of will, eros, and language back into the culture from which they arose and, in his view, to which they belonged" ("A-Morality" 21). A "grim necessity" forces Hester to put her cap and letter back on in the forest, and later to return to Massachusetts and resume the letter and her life of isolation. Who insists on this penance that "not the sternest magistrate of that iron period would have imposed"? The narrator tells us that she did it "of her own free will." But in a novel where freedom is ever and always reined in and put under a strict hand of control, we must ask what kind of free will this could be. It is a self-imposed, internalised discipline and punishment, a punishment and a discipline which the whole novel has taught us how to bear.[28] Bercovitch sees the novel "as a story of socialization, where the point of socialization is not to conform, but to consent. Anyone can submit; the socialized believe. It is not enough to have the letter imposed; you have to do it yourself ("A-Politics" 630).

The novel, then, would teach us not just sympathy but discipline, control, and denial as well. I have tried to show how these two seemingly contrasting impulses are intertwined in *The Scarlet Letter*. The novel, Bercovitch argues, teaches us how to seek and want this discipline for ourselves. In that sense it teaches us a form of masochism, teaches us to desire pain. It effects this, at least in part, through the construction of Dimmesdale's own desires.

What does a woman want? asked Freud. The answer in *Clarissa* – at least according to Lovelace – was that she wants to be raped. In this novel the more appropriate question might be, "What does Dimmesdale want?" and at least one answer would be that he wants what Hester has. He wants what she is wearing, and will go through extraordinary pain to get it. The whole story can be read as an account of Dimmesdale's struggle to get on the scaffold with Hester, to take her place. What I would suggest is that this great desire expressed (and repressed) by Dimmesdale to *take* Hester's place serves ultimately and paradoxically to keep her *in* her place. The position of shame, penance and humiliation is glorified through man's desire for it. Because a man desires it, because it brings attention, the *display* of pain, if not the actual pain itself, becomes desirable. The desire of another, the recognition of another, teaches us that pain brings attention and even a kind of love. The position of pain and display is once again marked as feminine.

Dimmesdale wants to be in two places at once. He wants to, or feels that he should, show God and society that his place is with Hester on the scaffold, but his status and career keep him from it. His awareness of his own hypocrisy ironically makes him a better speaker and a better minister. Just as the letter A gives Hester sympathetic knowledge of the guilty secrets of others, so Dimmesdale's sympathy for Hester and his unconfessed sin grant him almost hypnotic powers of persuasion and eloquence: "But this very burden it was, that gave him sympathies so intimate with the sinful brotherhood of mankind; so that his heart vibrated in unison with theirs, and received their pain into itself, and sent its own throb of pain through a thousand other hearts, in gushes of sad, persuasive eloquence. Oftenest persuasive, but sometimes terrible! The people knew not the power that moved them thus" (98). Suffering and guilt make good art. This much is standard Romantic doctrine. What I would like to suggest is that good art might also depend in this case upon a secret attachment to the victimization of woman, a longing to see her punished and to feel that punishment oneself.

Some recent criticim has focused on Hawthorne's gender-related anxiety of authorship. It has been suggested that Hawthorne, whom many of his friends claimed had "womanly" attributes,[29] worried that his chosen profession of writer was unmanly. This might help to explain his famous diatribe against female writers: "What a strange propensity it is in these scribbling women to make a show of their hearts, as well as their heads, upon your counter, for anybody to pry into that chooses."[30] Hawthorne's disgust and outrage stem from two sources. The first is the indecent exposure demonstrated in these writings. He dislikes their cheap, even promiscuous, availability, "for anybody to pry into that chooses."[31] The second is connected to the first. The desire to show oneself is considered a feminine trait (one that has to be continually opposed by the equally "feminine" trait of modesty). (In this sense Hawthorne reveals his kinship with earlier writers like Rousseau who associated acting and display with prostitution and femininity.) To keep things stoically "close to the chest" is the masculine way of doing things. Seen in this light, Dimmesdale's doomed attempt to hide his identification with Hester becomes a (doomed) attempt at masculinity.

Not only is the female considered to be the more expressive of the sexes; she is also the more decorated. It is the female who sports the finery and ribbons; the male adopts plainer dress. In this sense, Hester's embroidery of the letter is a feminization of it, made all the more striking in that it exists in the dull plain world of (masculine) Puritan dress: "It was so artistically done, and with so much fertility and gorgeous luxuriance of fancy" (39). The mark that Hester wears, therefore, comes to symbolize not only her own deviance/defiance versus the triumph of the law, but her sex as well. She is the sex which displays, the sex which shows. In wanting the mark of punishment on his breast, Dimmesdale wants not just the mark of guilt, but the mark of femininity as well.

Hester's position can thus be described as no more "full," no more "important" than Clarissa's. Each functions as a vessel through which identifications can be routed. The route of identification for the reader of *The Scarlet Letter* is as circuitous as ever. We feel through a male who wants to feel for, or "feel as," the heroine. Our attachment to Hester is built from a complex knot of sympathy, fear and guilt, its threads so intertwined as to be nearly indistinguishable.

4 Changing Places: Gender and Identity in *The Portrait of a Lady*

The *Portrait of a Lady*, like *Clarissa* and *The Scarlet Letter*, presents us with the spectacle of a heroine – strong, energetic and virtuous – who is ultimately caught and imprisoned. Like Clarissa and Hester, Isabel Archer seems by the end of her novel unable to move or rescue herself. Others, however, are profoundly moved by her story, so that once again the story becomes as much about the heroine's ability to move others as it is about her, herself. As she moves others, so her novel moves us, and this is done, I will argue, through the creation and exploitation of twin desires: the first a desire to love and to pity, the second an avid desire to possess.

Clarissa we read as a school of sympathy and *The Scarlet Letter* as a school of sympathy and guilt. *The Portrait of a Lady* becomes a school of value. But whether our lesson is in the value of love and art or in the love and art of value is not entirely clear. In this novel, issues of value and commerce become confusingly entangled with issues of sympathy and love.

In his preface to *The American*, Henry James writes of the importance of anchoring the central consciousness of the novel in his hero, of getting, as it were, "inside his head": "For the interest of everything is all that it is *his* vision, *his* conception, *his* interpretation: at the window of his wide, quite sufficiently wide, consciousness we are seated, from that admirable position we 'assist.' He therefore supremely matters; all the rest matters only as he feels it, treats it, meets it."[1]

James insists (the emphases in the quoted passage are all his) on both Newman's absolute and unquestioned possession of "*his* vision, *his* conception," etc., *and* on our own attendance (assistance) within his consciousness. Why should James feel the need to stress the character's full proprietership if, at the same time, he is to invite us to stay? Could it be that the place which is so much "his" is exactly ours to possess? Could it be that Newman has been created, has been made to "supremely matter," so that we might have an "admirable position" from which to "assist," that he is nothing more than a site constructed for us – not merely to feel and to see from but also to occupy? The traditional analysis of James' celebrated use of point of view stresses the anchoring or centring of such a site as a structural solution to a structural problem.[2] But what is involved goes far beyond issues of form and structure to engage issues of subjectivity, gender, power, and control.[3]

James continues his analysis of our relationship to the hero of *The American* in this way: "A beautiful infatuation this, always, I think, the intensity of the creative effort to get into the skin of the creature; the act of personal possession of one being by another at its completest" (37). Dorrit Cohn claims that this passage is "probably the most direct allusion to the sexual act in his entire oeuvre" (115). It is certainly no structuralist description and is something more than a formal solution to a formal problem. Indeed, it seems to be a description of some kind of love affair. This "effort to get into the skin of" another, this "act of personal possession of one being by another," is heralded as being "creative" and "complete." The phrases are ripe with implications of sexuality and violence, though all such implications remain unacknowledged, even ignored, by the text. They are masked by other phrases such as "the creative effort" and "a beautiful infatuation." By describing the act of coming to possess another as "creative" and "beautiful," the author renders it aesthetic and nearly tame. Such a description does not, however, entirely solve James' problem. Naming this act of imagined possession an infatuation complicates rather than solves the issue. The *Shorter* OED (3rd ed.) tells us that an infatuation is that which renders one fatuous or silly. It is "an extravagantly foolish or unreasoning passion." In other words, the same aestheticization which was to have ennobled or sanctified a suspiciously violent and sexual act now threatens to trivialize the entire project.

This beautiful infatuation, this love affair, appears to be precariously balanced between two poles. On the one hand, there are clear indications of physicality, sexuality, and perhaps violence in the concepts of "getting into the skin of the creature" and "the act of personal possession of one being by another." On the other is the troubling implication (signaled by the word "infatuation") that the whole enterprise may be foolish and degrading. These are the polarities James seeks to bridge through aesthetics, by insisting that the entire project is "creative," and "beautiful." But the balance seems precarious, the foundation of his project insecure. The troublesome implications – sexuality, control, and violence on the one hand, and triviality, foolishness, and weakness on the other – remain in place. They remain and they disturb. Such is the anxiety of Henry James' art, an anxiety which is evident in *The Portrait of a Lady*. *The Portrait* works in, around, and through these tensions. It is a novel obsessed with the pleasures and trials of getting into the skin of another, and with the problems and necessity of identification and possession.

In his preface written some twenty-six years after the novel was first published, James appears to have recognized these problems. There he frets a great deal about "the possible limitations of my subject" (11), worrying that it is too "slight," "slim," or "thin" (8), too "frail" or "weak" (10).[4] This inadequate subject is, of course, Isabel Archer. The "wonder" as James puts it, is that "the Isabel Archers, [of this world] and even much smaller, female fry, insist on mattering" (9).

James's charge as an artist in general, and in this novel in particular, is to show that such small female fry can and do matter. He worries, however, that in paying attention to "this slight 'personality,' the mere slim shade of an intelligent but presumptuous girl" (8), he might appear to be acting foolishly and with "extravagance" (9), making an "ado" about nothing: "The novel is of its very nature an 'ado,' an ado about something, and the larger the form it takes the greater of course the ado. Therefore, consciously, that was what one was in for – for positively organising an ado about Isabel Archer" (9).

James is drawing our attention to what he sees as a large and rather awesome discrepancy, the gulf between the slimness and frailty of his subject – in this case a presumptuous girl affronting her destiny, but then he says, "Millions of presumptuous girls ... daily affront their destiny" (9) – and the greatness of his artistic mastery. The wonder, as he sees it, is that such a "small corner-stone" should come "to be [such] a square and spacious house" (8). He may, in other words, have been foolish to start with such a frail subject, but just look at what he has been able to do with it!

An infatuation, we remind ourselves, is constructed out of a similar sort of discrepancy. It is "an extravagantly foolish or unreasoning passion," or, as Webster's puts it, "a strong and unreasoning attachment esp. to something unworthy of attachment" (*Third New English Dictionary*, 1976). What is foolish about an infatuation – what makes the lover so "fatuous" – is the lack of proportion between the strength of his or her attachment and the weakness or insufficiency of the beloved. James, it would seem, is pointing to a similar lack of proportion. In a move that is at once self-mocking and self-aggrandizing, he wonders at the artistry which could have produced an "ado" so grand out of a subject so "frail." That artistry is presented here as a type of infatuation, a kind of love affair, that both ennobles and demeans. James' task is to convince us of the value of his effort. If, as the dictionary suggests, an infatuation is "extravagantly" foolish, it may be that James wants us to splurge along with him, or to reassure him at least that his expense, his "extravagance," is justified.

In order to read this novel correctly, the reader must be taught to "appreciate" and to value Isabel.[5] We are to be taught to care for her as an owner or collector might care for a possession of great value which few save the connoisseur can appreciate. We must recognize Isabel's frailty and weakness, and then love her in spite of them.[6] We must want to protect and possess her, must appreciate her both *because of* and *in spite of* her imperfections. James makes this explicit in the text of the novel. There he fondly lists her shortcomings, "her meagre knowledge, her inflated ideas," and worries that considering all these, "she would be an easy victim of scientific criticism if she were not intended to awaken on the reader's part an impulse more tender and more purely expectant" (54). That tender impulse must be something akin to sympathy or love. In the traditional way, it is called for as a bridge of understanding, an antidote to cold "scientific" judgment.[7]

About this passage Richard Poirier has written: "This exhortation is full of very strong feeling. The abrupt and overlapping changes of tone indicate James's anxious desire to convince the reader that for all the oddities he may see in Isabel, he is to love her

the more and to engage the less in any attempt to sum her up"
(207).[8] Poirier, like many other critics, emphasizes James' fondness
for Isabel. He notes his "anxious desire" that we come close and
"love" her, that we not stand back and objectify her, in an "attempt
to sum her up." While he is essentially correct that we readers build
our own relationship to both heroine and text following James'
lead, I think he has overlooked or oversimplified the text's more
complicated vision of Isabel. We *are* taught to love her, but our love
is not unproblematic. Some of those problems are hinted at in the
very fuss the author makes about her imperfections. Furthermore,
our love is troubled by anxieties about possession and degradation.
Much of this is evident in the collector/dealer theme explicated in
the preface.

Here James seems to underscore the possessive nature and moral
uncertainty of his aesthetic project. He calls his choice of a subject
"my grasp of a single character – an acquisition … I was, as seemed
to me, in complete possession of it" (7). He continues: "The figure
has to that extent, as you see, *been* placed – placed in the imagination that detains it, preserves, protects, enjoys it, conscious of its
presence in the dusky, crowded, heterogeneous back-shop of the
mind very much as a wary dealer in precious odds and ends, com-
petent to make an 'advance' on rare objects confided to him, is conscious of the rare little 'piece' left in deposit … and which is already
there to disclose its merit afresh as soon as a key shall have clicked
in a cupboard door" (8). What makes this passage remarkable is
the extent to which the novelist is willing to depict himself in an
unfavourable light. Indeed he seems almost to relish his own ghoul-
ish description of the relationship between author and subject. The
way he describes it, the novelist's imagination becomes something
like a china cabinet or prison. The subject, in this case "a certain
young woman affronting her destiny," becomes a pet, an object, a
"rare little 'piece'" for the novelist to detain, preserve, protect, and
enjoy. Kept in a cupboard, it is taken out occasionally to be fon-
dled, appreciated, and then returned.

Many have noted that James' portrait of Isabel Archer was to
some extent based on his cousin, Minnie Temple, and it may be that
we can trace some of the origins of James's possessive anxieties to
his feelings for Minnie.[9] Alfred Habegger has recently pointed out
the "vampiristic … or is the better term necrophiliac" (143) nature
of the author's relationship to the memory of Minnie. He argues

that while James was infatuated with, and to some extent identified with his bright and unconventional cousin,[10] he nevertheless derived a certain satisfaction from her death: "The most challenging person he knew had now become a manipulable object" (145). Habegger bases his observation on James' letters to his family at the time of Minnie's death. It seems that James was quick to grab the "idea" of his cousin, an "intelligent but presumptuous girl," and see what he could do with her. In fact, he seems to have felt that he could do more with her than she might have been able to do with herself. He wrote to his brother: "The more I think of her the more perfectly satisfied I am to have her translated from this changing realm of fact to the steady realm of thought. There she may bloom into a beauty more radiant than our dull eyes will avail to contemplate."[11] This is a blatant aestheticizing of a relationship which we have every reason to believe was problematic. James goes on: "She was at any rate the helpless victim and toy of her own intelligence – so that there is positive relief in thinking of her being removed from her own heroic treatment and placed in kinder hands."[12]

With astonishing logic, James here insists that Minny was bad for herself, a "victim of her own intelligence."[13] Because of such self-destructive tendencies, she was apparently not to be trusted as author of her own life. Her cousin, Henry, was better suited for the job.[14] Her "own heroic treatment" of herself, we are given to understand, was exhausting, was asking too much. She needed to be "placed in kinder hands." Those hands are, of course, the author's and ultimately ours, as well. By removing her from her own heroic treatment, we all become rescuers of a sort, recuing her from herself. But what "heroic treatment" lies in store for her? Fictionalized, are her chances of escaping victimization any better?

In his preface, James writes that "the figure has to that extent, as you see, *been* placed – placed in the imagination that detains it." He goes on to "recall" "my pious desire but to place my treasure right" (8). The repetition of the verb "placed" seems to be more than mere coincidence. In the letter to his brother, we read that Minnie needed to die in order to be *placed* in kinder hands, and in the preface, that the author found his subject already *placed* in his detaining imagination. Is it a need to reciprocate, a desire to pass on the gift, that leads James to write that he wants "but to place my treasure right"? Just as *he* had received the treasure, so he seems to want to pass it on, but only under certain conditions. Again the image of the dealer is invoked to encompass this process of acquisition and exchange: "I quite remind myself thus of the dealer resigned not to 'realise,' resigned to keeping the precious object locked up indefinitely rather than commit it, at no matter what price, to vulgar hands" (8). Ours, we can assume, are the non-vulgar hands into which Isabel will be placed. Non-vulgar perhaps, but not entirely non-commercial. If we are to have or own her, we must appreciate her, must be instructed as to her value. She becomes a possession of great value which few save the connoisseur can appreciate. The connoisseur/dealer has such respect for the item he is handling that he feels it would be better to keep it (her?) locked up rather than to place it in the hands of those incapable of recognizing value.

The irony of this explicit imagery concerning dealers, collectors, and connoisseurs is, of course, that the author's attitude toward Isabel comes to differ little from Gilbert Osmond's own relationship to his wife.[15] Both care for her as an object one might want to possess. The only difference is that we are told that Osmond "hated" his wife while we are taught to love her as we possess her.

Ralph Touchett, who in many ways serves as a surrogate for both author and reader, is explicitly compared to Osmond, as a connoisseur. Their similarities are noted, but then rigorously denied: "Ralph had something of this same quality, this appearance of thinking that life was a matter of connoisseurship; but in Ralph it was an anomaly, a kind of humorous excrescence, whereas in Mr Osmond it was the keynote, and everything was in harmony with it" (225). Ralph is excused on the grounds that he is a less thoroughgoing connoisseur than Osmond, whereas it is precisely Osmond's overwhelming connoisseurship which constitutes his villainy.[16]

If James takes such pains to differentiate the two men's modes of appreciation, it may be that, in considering the attributes of a connoisseur, he is confronting issues crucial to the definition of his own art. The idea of a connoisseur encompasses many of the tensions and polarities out of which that art developed. These are the same tensions we identified earlier: a possessiveness or proprietorship so fierce as to be nearly violent and sexual, versus a fear of triviality, foolishness, and degradation. Many of these tensions can be approached and understood through the term "value."

In the most general sense, a connoisseur is one who knows. In

James' work, however, where the term is almost always connected to other terms such as "dealer," "collector," or "proprietor," a connoisseur is one with a special type of knowledge. He is one who knows *value*. If we think for a moment about the work of a collector or dealer of rare objects, we can see that success depends upon a lag between the dealer's recognition of value and the public's. The successful dealer sees value in something that has been overlooked by others. Sometimes it is the dealer or connoisseur's superior knowledge and taste that provides this advantage, but sometimes it is just a matter of fashion, luck, and timing. If the dealer holds onto the piece, the price may increase. In his desire to detain it, preserve, protect, and enjoy it, James reports that "I quite remind myself of the dealer resigned not to 'realise.'" The dealer's profit is based on the precise manipulation and exploitation of the gap or lag between his knowledge and taste and the public's. The superiority and prescience of his knowledge bring him profit. Confident that others will eventually come to see the object as he does, he holds onto it. But what if the object is never perceived as valuable? If the dealer can never realise his profit? This seems to be a real worry for James (hence the frettings in the preface over his "slim," his "inadequate," his "weak" subject). If others fail to see the worth of the object, not only does the dealer never realise his profit, but he runs the further and more personal risk of appearing foolish, infatuated, and ridiculous. Only if others come to see as he does will he be able to realise his investment. Hence we have the author's anxious need to educate us as to Isabel's value, to teach us to appreciate her.[17]

James feels he has to teach us to value Isabel before he can "place [his] treasure right," both because of his love for the object and his need to "realise" his investment. There is, however, another sense in which James sees his role as one involving value. Captivating as the image of dealer/connoisseur may be, it does not tell the entire story. For James claims to have done more than just detain, preserve and protect his rare little piece; he wants us to see that he has *made* something out of her too. He is the one who has constructed the "square and spacious house" on the "small cornerstone." It is he who has "positively organiz[ed] an ado about Isabel Archer," he who has translated Minnie/Isabel "from this changing realm of fact to the steady realm of thought." This shift of emphasis from collector-connoisseur to creator implies a shift for the reader as well, leading us to ask: which are we to admire most, the girl or the master, the "slight personality" or the masterful "portrait" that has been made of it?[18]

Value is, by its very nature, contractual. As long as it depends upon market and exchange, value can never be determined by any single individual. The readers of *The Portrait of a Lady* are called upon to establish and work within just such a contract. This "contract" makes our work as active as it is passive. We are asked not only to sit back and appreciate Isabel like spectators at a drama, but also, in the very process, to determine the value of both Isabel Archer *and* the book Henry James has written about her. This enterprise is all the more difficult in that we are being asked to apply value to love and art, which are traditionally thought to be above such crass categorizations.

It is through the figure of Ralph that we first learn to appreciate Isabel and recognize her worth. Through his experience, we can trace both the problems and pleasures of identification in this novel. His "beautiful infatuation" with his spirited cousin leads him to attempt to live his life through hers. What this vicarious experience becomes, dangerously, is "the act of personal possession of one being by another at its completest," a possession at once sexual and artistic, bringing with it the troublesome implications discussed earlier – sexuality, control, and violence, on the one hand, and triviality, foolishness, and weakness on the other. These are Ralph's problems, but they become ours as well. Since Ralph serves as our eyes and our consciousness, he comes to stand in for both reader and author and thus to personify and exemplify the thrills and the dangers of reading, of writing, of *living* in novels. His relationship to Isabel represents in microcosm both the author's and the reader's troubled relationship to the heroine. There are many characters who seek to watch, know, and love Isabel, but among these, Ralph is pre-eminent. The entire novel is almost exactly framed by his sight of her. It opens on the day he meets her at Gardencourt and ends a few days after his death. His is the central consciousness, the main pair of eyes, to regard and appreciate Isabel. Others, such as Lord Warburton, Caspar Goodwood, Henrietta Stackpole, and Mr and Mrs Touchett, serve as something like his alter-egos, providing shadings and variations on his concentrated and unifying focus.

One reason that the figure of Ralph is so important is that in this, as in all the other novels considered in this study, we cannot study the heroine without studying our response to her. Ralph focuses that response. We feel, see, and respond through him. The story in *The Portrait* gets displaced, just as it did in *Clarissa* and *The Scarlet Letter*, from a focus on the heroine herself to the circle of spectators (Ralph and others) who surround her. This creates a kind of double gaze. We join those characters in the novel who watch, *and* we watch them in turn as we read about them. The response to the heroine is thus both created and displayed.

These positions of watching and being watched are not, however, power neutral. Each brings with it a different amount of freedom or containment. As the heroine/victim comes to move less and less, those who watch are "moved" more and more. As the constraints on her freedom are increased, so is our emotional response. In this way, Isabel Archer's role is strikingly similar to that of Clarissa Harlowe and Hester Prynne. As the heroines' own sphere of influence and freedom shrinks, ours – at least initially – expands, and our emotional range and response feel like a kind of freedom. The question we must ask is, To what extent does this sense of freedom depend upon the representation of the imprisonment of others? As Ralph himself wryly puts it to Isabel as he lies on his death bed, "There's nothing makes us feel so much alive as to see others die" (477).

When Ralph is first introduced, he is described as having a "mind ... which, naturally inclined to adventure and irony, indulged in a boundless liberty of appreciation" (43-4). Later he is referred to as "an apostle of freedom" (386). In a novel as concerned as this with issues of freedom and containment, we must take notice of such phrases. Ralph may himself be constrained by limitations in health and strength, but he seeks to make up for these by becoming an observer: "The simple use of his faculties became an exquisite pleasure; it seemed to him the joys of contemplation had never been sounded" (46). His is a boundless liberty which we, as readers, are invited to share. It is not, however, a liberty that either we or Ralph can enjoy for long.

While we have seen how this symbiotic relationship of freedom and arrest works in *Clarissa* and *The Scarlet Letter*, Isabel Archer's plight seems particularly poignant. No other heroine is so pointedly and determinedly committed to freedom. Isabel is defined by her need for independence. One of her very first assertions is to declare,

"I'm not a candidate for adoption ... I'm very fond of my liberty" (30). It is this love of freedom that makes her eventual (spiritual) incarceration so horrifying. When she assesses her marriage during her long night's vigil in chapter 42, she realizes that "Instead of leading to the high places of happiness, from which the world would seem to lie below one, so that one could look down with a sense of exaltation and advantage, and judge and choose and pity, it [her marriage] led rather downward and earthward into realms of restriction and depression where the sound of other lives, easier and freer, was heard as from above, and where it served to deepen the feeling of failure" (356). She who had loved freedom to such an extent that she had turned from Caspar Goodwood because "he seemed to deprive her of the sense of freedom" (104-5), and who had refused Lord Warburton's offer of marriage because it didn't conform to her idea of "the free exploration of life" (101), is eventually confined to walls which "were to surround her for the rest of her life. It was the house of darkness, the house of dumbness, the house of suffocation" (360).

This is the central paradox of *The Portrait of a Lady* – that a heroine so gifted and so free should end up so imprisoned and bound. She was, after all, as Ralph puts it, "The last person I expected to see caught ... to be put into a cage" (288). How does this come to be? She herself has declared, "I shall not be an easy victim" (144). Neither was Clarissa or Hester, and yet each is caught. But Isabel's plight appears the most baffling. Unlike Clarissa, she has neither a villainous brother nor a Lovelace to trap her. Unlike Hester, she has no grim Puritanical laws to blame. She can *only* blame herself. She thinks: "It was impossible to pretend that she had not acted with her eyes open; if ever a girl was a free agent she had been. A girl in love was doubtless not a free agent; but the sole source of her mistake had been within herself. There had been no plot, no snare; she had looked and considered and chosen" (340).[19]

How does it come to be that a heroine so gifted and freedom-loving should end up so imprisoned and bound, and with only herself to blame? While some commentators have attempted to answer this question by focusing on Isabel's individual psychological characteristics and motives, and have analyzed her as if she were a real person, it is equally important to consider what might be at stake in writing and reading a novel in which the heroine is shown to both make and return to her own prison so willingly. This consideration leads me to look not so much to the heroine herself as to the actual process of reading and writing about such a heroine. Like Hester in *The Scarlet Letter*, Isabel apparently returns "of her own free will" to the site of her oppression, and seeks her own confinement. In both cases we have to wonder why, and what lesson we are meant to learn from this.

Others have wondered at Isabel's seemingly voluntary curtailment of her own liberty in which she refuses all offers of help and release, returning, apparently, to Italy and her marriage. Richard Poirier, one of James' best critics, tries to understand the ending by claiming: "There can be no such thing as the 'freedom' which Isabel wants and which Ralph and James want for her, simply for the reason that regardless of opportunity in the world outside, there are in everyone the flaws, the fears, the neuroses that fix and confine and stifle" (207).

Although he is entirely correct to say that Isabel is "fix[ed], confine[d] and stifle[d]," Poirier locates these forces inside each and every one of us. By contrast he sees the "world outside," as holding "opportunity," and hence freedom. But what if it is that very world – society and its novels – that *creates* those confining and stifling fears, creates them so that they reside – or appear to reside – "inside" us? Poirier, like others before him, seeks a reason for Isabel Archer's ending up as she does, and seeks it in the "inside" of the character. This self-destructive interior confounds every desire on the part of character, author, and we may presume, reader, for escape, freedom, and happiness. I want to shift our gaze away from the heroine's interiority, which critics seem to forget is "only fiction," and look instead at the processes of reading and writing themselves. I see these as processes which not only teach us (and perhaps particularly teach the females among us) "the fears ... that fix and confine and stifle," but also make these fears palatable and even attractive.

We have already discussed ways in which our relatively free position as readers seems to depend upon the "arrest" of the heroine, but there is a sense in which writing itself seems to depend upon a similar "fixing." James seems to be aware of this connection when he writes in the preface about his construction of "the large building of 'The Portrait of a Lady.' It came to be a square and spacious house ... but, such as it is, it had to be put up round my young woman while she stood there in perfect isolation" (8). James' house comes to differ little from Gilbert Osmond's house of dumbness and suffocation. The construction of his large and spacious house appears to rely on a heroine who must be isolated, held still. That this is an irony of which the author seems aware, and ready to play on throughout the novel, makes it no less horrifying.

Ironically, it is Isabel's great love of freedom, along with her indomitable will and self-sufficiency, which make her so desirable to others. These are the qualities that attract lovers and friends and that make her so valuable, make her such a prize specimen for a collection. Throughout *The Portrait* there is a recurring gesture to appropriate, take care of, or "adopt" Isabel, accompanied by her equally frequent gesture of refusal. Indeed, her character comes to be defined by her rejection of others' embraces (Mrs Touchett's, Lord Warburton's, Caspar Goodwood's, and even Henrietta's). It is her apparent self-sufficiency which attracts Ralph, who seeks "the thrill of seeing what a young lady does who won't marry Lord Warburton" (133). Like Lovelace, he wants to discover the nature of the heroine's desire, to discover for himself what it is that she *really wants*.

In *Clarissa* Lovelace's need to discover the secret of female desire was expressed in the form of a trial. In *The Scarlet Letter* the focus was less on the mystery of female desire than on Dimmesdale's desire to identify with female shame and display. In *The Portrait* Ralph's experiment seems, by contrast, more benign, even magnanimous. He wants to set Isabel free, to leave her entirely in command of herself so as to see what she will do, whom or what she will choose if she is completely unfettered.[20] He thinks Isabel is a good candidate for such an experiment because she already appears to be remarkably self-sufficient: "But what was she going to do with herself? This question was irregular, for with most women one had no occasion to ask it. Most women did with themselves nothing at all; they waited in attitudes more or less gracefully passive, for a man to come that way and furnish them with a destiny. Isabel's originality was that she gave one an impression of having intentions of her own. 'Whenever she executes them,' said Ralph, 'may I be there to see!'" (64).

"The impossible place of female desire," is Teresa de Lauretis's phrase (*Alice* 69). Theorists like de Lauretis and Irigaray have written about the denial of woman's desire in our culture, the impossibility of claiming a desire of one's own. In this novel, Henry James seems to be trying to call that desire into existence, attempting to represent what it might look like. Should we be surprised to learn that, once again, the heroine chooses confinement and pain "of her own free will"?[21]

Ralph wants to set Isabel free for two connected, although contradictory, reasons. The first is love, his "beautiful infatuation," with Isabel. The second, inspired to a large degree by that love, is Ralph's desire to live *through* Isabel. He can both create her by giving her a lot of money (and in that sense becoming her author), and then live through his creation (and in that sense exist as a reader). Just as James spoke in his preface to *The American* of providing us with a consciousness (Newman's) which we might possess ("at the window of his wide, quite sufficiently wide, consciousness we are seated"), Isabel provides Ralph with a life he can live, a consciousness (if not a body) that he can possess.

The relationship sketched between reader and character in the preface to *The American* is, I would argue, the same as that between Ralph and Isabel. He creates her so that he might live through her, so that he might have something to "read." She has *almost* everything a young woman could want. She is pretty, lively, clever and good. Ralph wants to finish her by making her rich.[22] In this sense, by freeing and "finishing" Isabel much as James did with his cousin, he is more author than reader.[23] But it may be that he becomes an author only to have something interesting to read. As Ralph explains to his father, "I take a great interest in my cousin ... but not the sort of interest you desire. I shall not live many years; but I hope I shall live long enough to see what she does with herself" (160). His father wonders at this: "'You speak as if it were for your mere amusement.'

"'So it is, a good deal.'

"'Well, I don't think I understand,' said Mr Touchett with a sigh'" (161).

Later, his father adds, "Well I don't know ... I don't think I enter into your spirit. It seems to me immoral" (162).

If Isabel is a kind of aesthetic project for Ralph, the father warns that such a project might at the very best be trivial – "mere amusement" – and at the very worst be immoral. These warnings echo James' own doubts about his artistic project, voiced in the preface to *The American*. There we saw that he was haunted by the twin doubts that the project of aesthetic identification might involve feelings of violent and/or sexual possession or, even worse, prove to be nothing more than a foolish triviality. These twin doubts continue to haunt Ralph and *The Portrait*. Ralph seems to deal with his anxiety by alternating between first idealizing and aggrandizing and then objectifying and belittling his project. When he thinks of Isabel, he seems ambivalent as to her value: "He wondered whether he were harbouring 'love' for this spontaneous young woman from Albany; but he judged that on the whole he was not ... Lord Warburton had been right about her; she was a really interesting little figure" (63).

It is in language reminiscent of a dealer or collector that Ralph describes his feelings for Isabel. She is a figure, little but interesting. The double insistence on *both* her insubstantiality *and* on her "interest" or "value" to those in the know runs throughout the book. When Ralph experiences doubts about his project, he evaluates her in the same terms: "If his cousin were to be nothing more than an entertainment to him, Ralph was conscious she was an entertainment of a high order" (63). The gesture should by now seem familiar. We have a double bind in which the object of attention or desire is simultaneously valued and devalued, is called "an interesting little figure," "a rare little piece," (first valued, then devalued) or, as in this example, "an entertainment of a high order," in which something that is usually of little value is exalted.

Other characters wonder about the purpose of Ralph's undertaking. Henrietta, like Mr Touchett, has her suspicions about the nature of Ralph's attachment to Isabel. When she speaks to Ralph of her fears for Isabel, she says, " 'What I'm afraid of is that she'll injure herself.'

" 'I think that's very possible,' said Ralph.

" '... That too would amuse you, I suppose' " (108).

Even Isabel uses the word "amuse" as accusation: "Is that why your father did it – for your amusement?" (192). Later, when Ralph learns of her impending marriage, he replies to her in this fashion: " 'I had treated myself to a charming vision of your future,' Ralph observed ... 'I had amused myself with planning out a high destiny for you. There was to be nothing of this sort in it. You were not to come down so easily or so soon ... It hurts me,' said Ralph audaciously, 'hurts me as if I had fallen myself!'

"The look of pain and bewilderment deepened in his companion's face. 'I don't understand you in the least,' she repeated. 'You say you amused yourself with a project for my career – I don't understand that. Don't amuse yourself too much, or I shall think you're doing it at my expense' " (291).

From this passage it is apparent that there are two dangers in the kind of aesthetic projection or identification Ralph has undertaken. The first is that he lays himself open to the charge that it is trivial, foolish, a mere amusement or entertainment. The second is that this mere amusement, something which seemed to offer "a boundless liberty of appreciation," can lead to pain. "It hurts me," he claims, "hurts me as if I had fallen myself." Part of the nature of this pain stems from the sense that his liberty and his amusement were at another's expense.[24] Ralph offers his hurt as evidence of his own innocence. The pain, he feels, should prove him innocent of exploitation. The pain should absolve him of the charge that he has been using Isabel for his own enjoyment.

Ralph, like Caspar Goodwood, has "invested his all in [Isabel's] happiness" (405) and future. The investment of oneself in another, this type of "beautiful infatuation," is embarked upon by not only Ralph, but by almost every other character in *The Portrait*. It is also the kind of investment required of a reader. Ralph is the central instance of this type of identification or living through another, but there are many more.

At the beginning of the novel old Mr Touchett complains to his son of a lack of feeling in his legs. " 'Perhaps some one might feel for you,' said the younger man, laughing." To which his father replies, "Oh I hope some one will always feel for me!' " (20). Just as this play on words indicates, "to feel for someone" has two meanings. While its usual sense is to experience love or sympathy, it can also mean to do the feeling for, to feel in the place of. Both senses are explored in *The Portrait*.

James' novel is characterized by an astonishing number of characters who, in one way or another, want to feel for, or change places with, one another. From our first glimpse of Lord Warburton, who "had a certain fortunate brilliant exceptional look ... which would have made almost any observer envy him ... [and] have provoked you to wish yourself almost blindly, in his place," (19) to the machinations of Madame Merle who wishes to install Isabel in her place as the wife of Osmond and mother of Pansy, characters are involved in complex and sometimes contradictory transactions of substitution and displacement. They attempt in various ways to live in and through one another. Ralph is thus not the only character to attempt to live *through* another, to try to feel for and through another. Ralph may use Isabel to feel for him, to love for him, to marry for him,[25] but almost all the characters in this novel use each other in similar ways.

This novel about reading and writing as forms of identification offers several methods of putting oneself in the place of the other. The simplest and most straightforward of these appears to be envy. Envy, as James puts it, provokes "you to wish yourself almost blindly in [another's] place." It is an acknowledgment of the other's superior "value" or worth in relation to one's own.

Pity, while seeming to be the nobler emotion, is also based on an evaluation of the comparative status of two individuals. To pity another is to set oneself above, to value one's own position over that of the other. Pity and envy, apparent opposites, are frequently linked in this novel, pointing perhaps to the uncertain and fluid nature of value relations within it. Exchange, acquisition, and commerce: the economy of this book – its work of substitution and dispacement – depends upon the continuous exchange of one thing for another along with the continuous assessment of each item's worth.

Pity and envy become, then, not so much opposites as two sides of the same coin. One cannot exist without the other. We have seen that Lord Warburton was introduced as a man "almost any observer [would] envy" or would wish to take the place of. Very quickly, however, this characterization of the man is modified. Isabel asks the senior Mr. Touchett, "'But you don't pity Lord Warburton then as Ralph does?' Her uncle looked at her a while with genial acuteness. 'Yes, I do, after all!'" (73). The theme is repeated in a conversation among Isabel, Osmond, and Ralph about the same individual: "'That's a man I could envy.'

"Isabel considered him with interest. 'You seem to me to be always envying some one ...'

"'My envy's not dangerous ... I only want to *be* them ... But why' – Osmond reverted – 'do you speak of your friend as poor?'

"'Women . . . sometimes pity men after they've hurt them; that's their great way of showing kindness,' said Ralph" (256). It seems that one must pity Lord Warburton just as surely as one must envy him. Although conventionally defined as opposites, envy and pity serve the same purpose; they allow one to imagine oneself, however briefly, in the place of the other.

The way that Isabel "feels for" Pansy seems to be another instance of that curious hybrid of pity and envy: Pansy's "spark of timid passion touched Isabel to the heart. At the same time a wave of envy passed over her soul, as she compared the tremulous longing, the definite ideal of the child with her own dry despair. 'Poor little Pansy!' she affectionately said" (440). A final example is one of Ralph's many assessments of his relationship to Isabel. "'No, I don't think I pity her,' he claims. 'She doesn't strike me as inviting compassion. I think I envy her'" (46).

Whether it is pity, envy, or some other relationship, the fact remains that the invalid Ralph wants and needs to use Isabel to feel for him. The novel explores the dangers and the thrills of such a relationship. The characters' attempts to live through one another give the reader access to all. Our own identification is facilitated by the slippages between the characters. Pity and envy act as lubricants easing the way for us (characters within the novel and readers without) to imagine ourselves as another. The effect may be exhilarating; we are after all safely allowed to take masculine *and* feminine positions, play spectator *and* spectacle. But the exhilaration does not last. We the readers are left, I would sugggest, feeling confined and helpless rather than liberated and powerful.[26]

Richard Poirier claimed that Isabel was bound to fail because of the fears that confine and stifle us all. Are those fears passed on to the reader as well? When Ralph learns of Isabel's impending marriage to Gilbert Osmond, he says that "it hurts." "'It hurts me,' said Ralph audaciously, 'hurts me as if I had fallen myself'" (291). His assertion is "audacious" in that it claims to be able to know and experience the feelings or pain of another. It is the audacity of "the beautiful infatuation," in which one tries "to get into the skin of the creature." It is audacious for Ralph or *anyone* to claim that he or she can feel the pain that another feels. Such is the audacity of art.

The pain that Ralph claims as his own is, however, not the only emotion with which the reader is left. Witnessing Isabel's pain brings with it a sense of hopelessness as well, a feeling of resignation and powerlessness that all of those surrounding Isabel feel. When Henrietta informs Isabel that she will be leaving Italy in order to accompany the dying Ralph back to England, she says to Isabel:

> 'I see you want us all to go. I don't know what you want to do.'
>
> 'I want to be alone,' said Isabel.
>
> 'You won't be that so long as you've so much company at home.'
>
> 'Ah, they're part of the comedy. You others are spectators.'
>
> 'Do you call it a comedy, Isabel Archer?' Henrietta rather grimly asked.
>
> 'The tragedy then if you like. You're all looking at me; it makes me uncomfortable.'
>
> Henrietta engaged in this act for a while. 'You're like the stricken deer, seeking the innermost shade. Oh, you do give me such a sense of helplessness!' she broke out. (417)

To the very end Isabel seeks the shade that will shield her from the view of the spectators. Their view of her life as tragedy makes her "uncomfortable." Just as Clarissa wanted to slide through life unnoted and Hester seeks refuge in the forest or in Europe, so Isabel must hide. The heroines seek refuge from the glare of the attention trained upon them, from the gazes not just of all the characters within the novels who, like Henrietta, stare sympathetically and helplessly, but from our own gaze as well. We, the readers, stare along with the sympathizing spectators in the novel, until Isabel literally vanishes at the end of the novel. Her virtue and her desirability depend upon her sense of modesty and independence. Our pleasure and our pain depend, helplessly, on her victimization.

5 "A Thousand Pities":
The Reader and
Tess of the d'Urbervilles

In one of the best recent readings of *Tess of the d'Urbervilles*, J. Hillis Miller repeatedly asks one question. "Why," he wonders, "does Tess suffer so?" (*Fiction and Repetition* 140). His own deconstructive answer, while insightful and meticulously drawn, remains unsatisfactory. He claims there is no "single accounting cause" (141) for her suffering, and instead identifies a pattern built up out of chains of signification, each referring and deferring to another: "None of these chains has priority over the others as the true explanation of the meaning of the novel" (126). True as it may be that the novel's meaning cannot be isolated in any one strand or theme, Miller's analysis leaves a large question unanswered. If *Tess* is nothing more than a pattern of repetitions, is "only an endless sequence of them, rows and rows written down" (141), then how do we account for its emotional power?

Miller returns to this when he writes that "no good reader of *Tess of the d'Urbervilles* can fail, in his or her turn, to be deeply moved by the novel ... I for one find the description of Angel Clare's failure to consummate his marriage to Tess almost unbearably painful" (119). A British critic, John Goode, has a similar reaction: "I have read and reread *Tess of the d'Urbervilles* many times during twenty years," he writes, "and I still find the end impossible to read" (*Thomas Hardy* 137).

Although each man chooses a different passage, the responses are remarkably similar. Both claim that a book about a woman's suffering is so painful as to be nearly unbearable. Their statements also imply that it is this pain – so intense as to threaten to disrupt the very reading process itself – which supplies the book with its emotional and moral greatness. Miller's question is, "Why does Tess suffer so." My question echoes his. Why does Miller suffer so? Why does the book demand such a response? What is this pain that makes the reader feel so bad and makes the book so good?

In the late 1920s, I.A. Richards taught *Tess of the d'Urbervilles* in China. When he read the tragic ending of that novel aloud to his students, the ending that John Goode cannot bear to read, the Chinese students reacted in the following way: "When Richards read the climactic lines, 'the President of the Immortals had ended his sport with Tess,' the class burst into spontaneous applause for the only time in the course. In a state of amazement Richards passed out protocols, and back came the universal response: Tess had shown disrespect for her father at the beginning of the novel. The students had been waiting for the just punishment that a great artist like Hardy would surely mete out."[1]

This is a far different reaction from those we have just considered. That the Chinese students appear to have felt elation and vindication, not pain, upon learning of Tess's fate demonstrates the culturally determined nature of Miller and Goode's responses to the novel. Miller will never find the answer to his question, "Why does Tess suffer so?" in his "chains of signification" so long as these chains are kept isolated from issues of power, gender, and culture. Nor, I suspect, would he be particularly eager to accept the answer provided by Richards' Chinese students that Tess suffers, that she *needs* to suffer, because she showed disrespect for her father early in the book. We cannot expect meaning to spring full blown from some innocent or culturally-neutral meeting of reader and text. Culture, language, politics: all of these at the very least *inform*, and at the very most *determine* how we read. The painful response experienced by Miller, Goode, and others cannot be considered as some private or personal response transcending history and culture. It must instead be studied as a cultural response to historical and cultural pressures of which this novel is just one instance.

Miller asks the right question, but looks for the answer in the wrong place. First, as mentioned above, his deconstructive method blinds him to pressures of history, culture, and gender. But further, his question obliges him to focus obsessively (as does the novel) on the heroine, thereby isolating her as an icon of virtue and pain. My own interest, as should be clear by now, is to ask the same question as Miller – Why does Tess suffer so? – but to adjust the focus so that our gaze rests not solely on the heroine herself, or even on the representation of that heroine, but on the reading process involving both reader *and* heroine. In that way, we may discover a connection between the representation of the heroine's pain and our resulting empathetic pain and aesthetic pleasure.

Although J. Hillis Miller's deconstructive analysis of *Tess* cannot (and, to be fair, does not seek to) account for the difference between the reaction of the Chinese students to Tess's fate and that of most readers in English departments in the West, he does acknowledge the existence of a "good" reader. This, we may presume, is someone who has been *taught* – through culture and history, as well as through reading novels – how to respond, how to read, correctly: "It is because all good readers of *Tess* would agree that Tess suffers and even tend to agree that she does not wholly deserve her suffering, and it is because all good readers of *Tess* share in the narrator's sympathy and pity for that suffering, that we care about the question of why Tess suffers so" (*Fiction and Repetition* 119–20).

The good reader cares about Tess because he or she has been taught to care. *Why* we should have been taught this lesson is less important than the structure of the lesson itself. How does a novel like *Tess of the d'Urbervilles* go about teaching us to "share in the narrator's sympathy and pity for [Tess's] suffering?" These lessons in sympathy interest me, not so much for the charity that they purport to teach as for the power relations of domination and submission which they conceal.

From its very beginning, this novel was structured around the response of its readers. Because of the controversies and difficulties Hardy faced in his attempts to publish *Tess* at first serially and later as a novel, he was forced to make several revisions. Mary Jacobus has shown how during the process he attempted to make Tess's character less sensual and more innocent in order to ward off accusations that as a fallen woman and murderess she was not fit to be a heroine. ("Tess's Purity" 318–38). In these revisions, the novel seeks to rescue Tess from our bad opinion.

Hardy's anxious and almost defiant attempt to secure the reader's good opinion of Tess led him to add the subtitle "A Pure

Woman Faithfully Represented," a move he later regretted since it only added fuel to the fire, infuriating more readers than it won (Jacobus 319). The subtitle is polemical, its intent didactic. Given the controversies and difficulties Hardy faced in his attempts to publish *Tess*, we may also assume that it is deliberately confrontational. It tells us that the novel will teach us how to recognize and distinguish a truly pure woman. The novel's own representation, it claims, is faithful; it expects our investment to be just as true. We are to be taught what true purity looks like and are expected to respond "faithfully" and sincerely in turn. In this way, Hardy guides and constructs readers' response. We are to assist him in recognizing purity where other people miss it. The project undertaken by author and reader is similar in this respect to that undertaken in *The Portrait*, in which we were instructed to recognize quality. Here we are to be taught how to see and distinguish a type of woman who is at best usually ignored, and at worst shunned and despised. This is a lesson in sympathy and spectatorship that is very different from that provided in *The Scarlet Letter*, where sympathy was organised away from sight, through hearing or feeling. In *Tess* the narrator seems to be telling us that looking, or at least being able to distinguish, is an essential first step toward understanding and sympathy.

Tess is in large part defined by her own unimportance. The narrator says of her: "She was not an existence, an experience, a passion, a structure of sensations, to anybody but herself. To all humankind besides Tess was only a passing thought."[2] While on the face of it this is simple common sense – she is, after all, the only one capable of feeling her own subjectivity; to anyone else she can only be an object – an element of pathos is built into the narrator's statement. The passage, in fact, is more plea than statement. We are not simply being told that no one cares for Tess but are being solicited to give Tess more than "only a passing thought," because no one else will. We are being asked to recognize her as "an existence, a passion, a structure of sensations," to feel with her, to feel *as* her. What does this recognition entail? On the one hand it would seem to entail a putting of ourselves into her place, an attempt at identification, since we have to learn from the "inside" what it means to be her, to see as she sees, to think as she thinks. In this sense we are encouraged to merge our own identities with her fictional one. On the other hand the pleading note, the strain of pathos, in the narrator's statement about Tess's lonely position creates and maintains distance. By being asked to pity Tess, we are kept on the outside. We are continually reminded that to most of the world she is a nonentity. In other words the novel is asking us to take up two positions at once. We are not only asked to imagine what Tess must feel and thus merge with her subjectivity but we are also expected to maintain our own distinct identity so that we might regard her as an object deserving pity. The novel is built around this dialectic of subject and object. It is organized around two compositional poles, the subjectivity constructed for the reader (self-sufficient, empathetic, and, as we shall see, to a large degree masculine), and the subjectivity that is constructed for Tess (a subjectivity in which she is more often constructed as object than subject). It is out of the vacillation between these two poles that the texture of the novel is woven.[3]

There are many similarities between this structure and those employed in *Clarissa*, *The Scarlet Letter*, and *The Portrait of a Lady*. In *Clarissa* the epistolary style allows us to move in and out of characters' consciousness in ways sometimes quite abrupt, to experience them, as it were, from the inside and out. Hawthorne, in *The Scarlet Letter*, insists on a distance between spectator and heroine. *The Portrait* constructs for us a kind of loving "appreciation" for Isabel that is based on seeing her as simultaneously "interesting" and "little." All these depend upon a dialectic of – in J. Hillis Miller's terms – distance and desire.[4] In none of the texts, however, is this dialectic presented in terms so explicitly erotic as in *Tess*.

All the other texts played with, and to some extent subverted, their own fascination with the eroticism of their subject matter, but in *Tess* that eroticism is front and centre. In *Clarissa* the primary image is of a trial of female desire. In *The Scarlet Letter* the image is of the circle, spectators drawn toward, and repulsed by, the mark of the woman's sin and her punishment. In *The Portrait* the imagery is organized around issues of acquisition, collection, and value. In *Tess*, the radical vascillation between subjectification and objectification heightens and foregrounds the eroticism. The heightening is effected from our knowing and seeing two ways at once, knowing Tess, as it were, both inside and out.

The novel, as I have said, can be read as an attempt to subjectify what appears to be an object, to remedy the fact that "she was not an existence, an experience, a passion, a structure of sensations, to anybody but herself."[5] The idea that she might lack a subjectivity of her own is presented as a horror that the novel can do nothing about. Instead, it can only use this horror to create a sense of pathos and thus heighten its own effects. Its attempted subjectification creates a new eroticized (and pathetic) object.[6] After all, the narratorial voice is clearly male while the object of its attention is female. Penny Boumelha notes that there is a "tension inherent in this androgynous mode of narration, which has as its project to present woman, 'pure woman', as known from within and without, explicated and rendered transparent. In short, she is not merely spoken by the narrator, but also spoken *for*" (120). It may be that any attempt to subjectify the object – any such move between the first and the third persons – becomes eroticized, but it must become especially so in a novel as sexually charged as this one.

Much of this process of alternating subjectification and objectification is organized through scenes of visualization. The subjectification of Tess is a visualization of Tess. The links in this novel between vision and emotion are stronger than in perhaps any of the other novels considered in this study.[7] Tess is presented as a figure of overlooked and undervalued purity and suffering. Her unimportance in the eyes of the world is stressed in order to heighten our response, make us look more carefully. This emphasis on her insignificance is linked to the same modesty, the same disinclination to court the regard of others, that we saw in Clarissa Harlowe, Hester Prynne, and Isabel Archer. This modesty, however, has the curious effect of calling attention to her. As the narrator puts it, "The eye returns involuntarily to [Tess] ... Perhaps one reason why she seduces casual attention is that she never courts it, though other women often gaze around them" (125). This is one of the paradoxes of *Tess*, that a heroine who does not want to be seen, should "seduce" attention precisely by seeking to avoid it.[8] This disinclination to be looked at is a signal that readers should see her as the "pure woman" the text tells us she is.

In a novel claiming to want to subjectify its main character, there are a surprising number of scenes organized around the visualization of Tess as an object. One of the most famous of these occurs when Tess first walks to Talbothay's dairy. It is in this scene that she is described as being "of no more consequence to the surroundings than [a] fly" (151). What makes this particular scene so shocking is that its harsh objectification of Tess comes so abruptly. Before this the reader's point of view had been structured through Tess's. We had been looking through her eyes and had been experiencing her sense of release and jubilation as she leaves a painful part of her life behind and heads for her new one. She feels drawn by "the irresistible, universal, automatic tendency to find sweet pleasure somewhere" (149). Following are some examples of the point of view constructed for us as Tess walks: "She found herself on a summit commanding the long-sought-for vale, the Valley of the Great Dairies" (147–8), "The bird's-eye perspective before her was not so luxuriantly beautiful, perhaps, as that other one which she knew so well; yet it was more cheering" (148). Our gaze, our point of view, is at one with Tess's, seeing through her eyes, feeling what she feels. That gaze, a "bird's-eye perspective," is panoramic and its view "commanding." All this brings with it a concomitant lifting of the emotions, a strengthening and a "cheering": "Either the change in the quality of the air from heavy to light, or the sense of being amid new scenes where there were no invidious eyes upon her, sent up her spirits wonderfully. Her hopes mingled with the sunshine in an ideal photosphere which surrounded her as she bounded along against the soft south wind. She heard a pleasant voice in every breeze, and in every bird's note seemed to lurk a joy" (149). Part of her sense of liberation is surely based on her sense of independence and her "command" of her own perspective. She can see far and wide and yet remain unseen herself. There are "no invidious eyes upon her" here. Unseen, she can "mingle" and merge with the sights and sounds which surround her. The sensuality of this passage is registered through Tess's senses. We merge with her. We hear the birds and appreciate the lightness of the air through her.

The narrative voice then shifts very slightly; the tone becomes more objective. No longer are we quite so centrally placed in the heroine's consciousness, but begin to move away from and outside of her. "Tess Durbeyfield," the passage continues, "then, in good heart, and full of zest for life, descended the Egdon slopes lower and lower towards the dairy of her pilgrimage" (151). While we continue – as in the first half of this sentence – to maintain our privileged knowledge of Tess's inner thoughts, we are also – as demonstrated in the second half of the sentence – allowed to move outside of Tess to see her actions. This slight externalization of the point of view is standard technique in omniscient narration. In no way, however, does it prepare us for the scene which follows: "Not quite sure of her direction Tess stood still upon the hemmed expanse of verdant flatness, like a fly on a billiard-table of indefinite length, and of no more consequence to the surroundings than that fly" (151).

The effect of such a description is cinematic.[9] It is as if the camera, which had been positioned very close to Tess so as to describe things she saw and felt from an intimate angle, had suddenly pulled back to a much wider angle, revealing her as a mere speck on the landscape. Coming down from the summit she loses her perspective, her sense of direction and with it, apparently, all sense of power, independence, and importance. The readers, however, have continued to maintain the privileged and "commanding" view which we had earlier shared with Tess. Her move away from what had been our shared perspective opens up a gap, a gap the text seems to find both lamentable and exciting. In *Thomas Hardy: Distance and Desire*, J. Hillis Miller remarks that: "Hardy is adept at making sudden relatively small shifts in perspective which put his reader virtually, though not actually, at an indefinite distance from events − as if they were suddenly seen through the wrong end of a telescope" (51). This shifting back and forth produces a kind of vertiginous horror. That to which we had been close, with which one had felt intimacy, has been abruptly pulled away and rudely objectified, defamiliarized to an insect. The reaction created is shock, certainly, but it is also pathos. The purpose of such a sudden reversal would seem to be to awaken in us a horror of the distance and objectification of Tess, to renew in us a desire to bridge that distance through sympathy and love.[10]

These sudden reversals occur in the other direction as well. In the following passage, also remarkably cinematic, the narrator directs our gaze toward a Tess so objectified as to be nearly indistinguishable, and then has us look beyond or inside that object-ness to find the life or subjectivity within. In contrast to the previous scene in which the "camera" of the narratorial gaze pulls back, this time the effect is like a "zoom in" for a close-up: "Thus Tess walks on; a figure which is part of the landscape; a fieldwoman pure and simple, in winter guise: a gray serge cape, a red woollen cravat, a stuff skirt covered by a whitey-brown rough wrapper, and buff-leather gloves. Every thread of that old attire has become faded and thin under the stroke of raindops, the burn of sunbeams, and the stress of winds.

There is no sign of young passion in her now ... Inside this exteri-or, over which the eye might have roved as over a thing scarcely percipient, almost inorganic, there was the record of a pulsing life" (388). What is remarkable about this passage is that although the text tells us that her exterior blurs her into the landscape, making her "a thing scarcely percipient, almost inorganic," the compulsive detailing of its description serves to particularize Tess and bring her into focus. The text dwells lovingly on the details of her dress and on the particular effects of the weather it tells us threaten to obscure her. If the text seems to linger over these things which almost dehu-manize its heroine, it is because they heighten the pathos. The more Tess suffers, the more she comes into focus, and the more we can feel. Our feelings of love or identification are constructed by seeing her thus objectified and dehumanized.

In all of these scenes, our lessons in caring are organized around lessons in seeing. In order to know how to feel for Tess, we first must learn to see her, to distinguish her. Hardy indicates that not everyone has the ability to do this. It is only the select few who are capable of appreciating Tess's beauty: "A small minority, mainly strangers, would look long at her in casually passing by, and grow momentarily fascinated by her freshness, and wonder if they would ever see her again; but to almost everybody she was a fine and pic-turesque country girl, and no more" (23). The reader is thus invoked as one of "a small minority, mainly strangers." Such flat-tery serves as a kind of positive reinforcement for us to continue being able to see and distinguish Tess.[11] Kaja Silverman notes that, in chapter 2, there is an "insistent anchoring" of vision "to a view-er, who assumes in turn the guise of a tourist, a landscape painter, and a random passer-by" (1). It is out of such descriptions that we, as readers, construct our own subject positions in the novel. It should also be noted, of course, that these labels (tourist and ran-dom passer-by) aptly describe the character of Angel Clare. It is, in fact, as if he enters the book to fill the position which the text has opened up for him. This is just the first of many instances in which the reader's identity is constructed along the same pattern as Angel's.

The scene in which Tess and Angel meet – or rather, more sym-bolically, do *not* meet – contains in microcosm elements which are to recur later in this tragedy. The scene also establishes our own and

Angel's position toward Tess and thus links the reader's gaze to Angel's, much as it was linked to Ralph's in *The Portrait* and Belford's in *Clarissa*.

When Angel first approaches the field where Tess and the other village women are dancing, he is accompanied by his two brothers. He is attracted by "the spectacle of a bevy of girls dancing without male partners," and like Ralph Touchett, is "amused." But his brothers object: "Dancing in public with a troop of country hoydens – suppose we should be seen!" (24). The brothers are unable to distinguish any individuals among the troop.

Later, the narrator will comment on just such an inability to see well or to distinguish. Of Angel he says, "He was ever in the habit of neglecting the particulars of an outward scene for the general impression" (170). This is the habit which the novel seeks to break in trying to teach us to recognize "a pure woman" against stereotype, and it is the breakdown of just this sort of "habit' which occurs at the dairy, allowing Angel to see and love Tess: "Without any objective change whatever, variety had taken the place of monotonousness. His host and his host's household, his men and his maids, as they became intimately known to Clare, began to differentiate themselves as in a chemical process. The thought of Pascal's was brought home to him: 'A mesure qu'on a plus d'esprit, on trouve qu'il y a plus d'hommes originaux. Les gens du commun ne trouvent pas de différence entre les hommes.' The typical and unvarying Hodge ceased to exist. He had been disintegrated into a number of varied fellow creatures" (169). This is just the sort of insight and ability to distinguish which the brothers lack and which it takes Angel some time to learn. They need to learn to particularize; their "sin" is overgeneralization or stereotyping. This, it would seem, is also the lesson Hardy wanted to teach his Victorian readers. His novel can be read as an attempt to portray Tess in a manner that would challenge the stereotype of the fallen woman.

On another occasion, when Angel and all the farm workers set out in the fields in an organized phalanx to seek and destroy garlic, these "differentiated" and "varied" individuals seem to regroup themselves into that undifferentiated mass apparently known as "Hodge": "Differing one from another in nature and moods so greatly as they did, they yet formed, bending, a curiously uniform row – automatic, noiseless; and an alien observer passing down the neighbouring lane might well have been excused for massing them as 'Hodge'" (197). In an earlier passage, we saw how the reader was constructed as one of "a small minority, mainly strangers." In this passage, the narrator evokes "an alien observer" who would "excusably" and, we can surmise, unavoidably fail to distinguish the farmworkers as individuals. The reader is that "alien observer," who is to be taught, like Angel, how to see and how to love.

Angel's task, in his first scene with Tess and then in the novel as a whole, is to single out, to notice, and to love Tess. It is his failure to accomplish this task that sets the tragedy in motion. It is of this that Tess accuses him, when during their engagement she asks, "Why didn't you stay and love me when I – was sixteen; living with my little sisters and brothers, and you danced on the green?" (280).

That scene, the dance on the green, prefigures his situation at Talbothay's. There also, Angel is for a while the only eligible male in a bevy of young women. At first the text tells us that it was "amusement" that drew him toward the girls on the green, but later it is termed "pity": " 'This is a thousand pities,' he said gallantly, to two or three of the girls nearest him, as soon as there was a pause in the dance. 'Where are your partners, my dears?' "(25). His gallantry recognized, a girl asks him to choose a partner himself: "The young man, thus invited, glanced them over, and attempted some discrimination; but as the group were all so new to him, he could not very well exercise it. He took almost the first that came to hand, which was not the speaker, as she had expected; nor did it happen to be Tess Durbeyfield" (25). Because they are all "so new to him," he is unable to discriminate as he later learns to do with the country folk at Talbothay's. As on so many other occasions in this novel, when Angel *is* finally able to distinguish Tess from the rest of the crowd, he is "too late":[12] "As he fell out of the dance his eyes lighted on Tess Durbeyfield, whose own large orbs wore, to tell the truth, the faintest aspect of reproach that he had not chosen her. He, too, was sorry then that, owing to her backwardness, he had not observed her; and with that in his mind he left the pasture" (25).

We might note that the text blames Tess; "her backwardness" appears to be as much at fault as Angel's lack of discrimination. But it is Tess's faint "reproach," along with Angel's own sense of being "sorry," that sets the tone for the rest of the story. Near the end of the novel he comes to realize that that which has "value in life was less its beauty than its pathos" (462).

The poignancy of the whole novel, that which makes it both

beautiful and "unbearable," is its pathos, its sense of missed opportunities, of everything in its world being slightly out of joint.[13] The cart goes off its track and Prince is speared by an oncoming mail-cart. Tess's letter of explanation to Angel never reaches him, but goes under the carpet. She walks all the way to see Angel's parents and then loses her nerve, her boots discovered by Mercy Chant. Angel finally returns to rescue her only to find that he is a few days "too late." Things go wrong by being ever so slightly "off." A small misstep has enormous repercussions, and at each turn Tess or Angel feels "sorry."

This is a novel full of regret, reproach, and self-blame. When Prince dies, Tess exclaims, "Tis all my doing – all mine! ... No excuse for me – none" (44). Of old Mr Clare, Angel's father, the narrator tells us that "his silent self-generated regrets were far bitterer than the reproaches which his wife rendered audible" (461). In Brazil Angel feels "a regret for his hasty judgment" (464), and when he receives Tess's letter accusing him of cruelty and injustice, he agrees: "It is quite true!" (499).

The tone of pathos, nostalgia, and regret, permeating the end of the novel, is first sounded at the end of the dancing on the green section. There, Angel rushes off to rejoin his brothers. When he has run some distance and gained elevation and perspective, he looks back. Most of the girls "seemed to have quite forgotten him already" (26). Having lost all consciousness of him, they also lose any traces of individuality or subjectivity which they once might have had. To Angel now they are merely "white figures": "All of them, except, perhaps, one. This white shape stood apart by the hedge alone. From her position he knew it to be the pretty maiden with whom he had not danced. Trifling as the matter was, he yet instinctively felt that she was hurt by his oversight ... he felt that he had acted stupidly" (26).

Finally Tess has been distinguished. There are at least three things to note here. The first, as already mentioned, is that such distinction comes "too late." The second is that it is her "hurt" as much as anything else that distinguishes her. What hurts her is Angel's lapse in attention. Throughout the novel, Tess draws attention because of her looks – her eyes and mouth are obsessively dwelt upon – but she is primarily marked by her suffering. It is her pain, our "instinctive" sense of her inward suffering, as much as her beauty, which sets her apart and distinguishes her.

The third point to be noted about this passage is that Angel registers Tess's hurt and feels regret from a distance. He looks down at her, "this white shape" and the other "white figures of the girls" from a rise. His insight into her feelings seems to depend on distance and elevation. At the end of the novel he has to go all the way to Brazil to come to appreciate her. Angel is a man who needs perspective to be able to see. The reader's position is built on a similar base. Our love, sympathy and pity depend upon our sense of distance.[14]

At this point in the novel, Angel fails his first task. He sees Tess, registers her hurt, feels that he has acted stupidly, but then reflects that "it could not be helped, and turning, and bending himself to a rapid walk, he dismissed the subject from his mind" (26). The novel may be read as an admonition to its readers not to make Angel's mistake. We are never to dismiss Tess from our minds. To him "she was but a transient impression, half forgotten" (57). Hardy makes it his project that she be more to us. She is to become "an existence, an experience, a passion, a structure of sensations."

Upon reaching Talbothay's, Tess meets Angel once again. Although at first he does not remember ever having seen her before, she remembers him. "Angel Clare rises out of the past not altogether as a distinct figure, but as an appreciative voice, [and] a long regard of fixed, abstracted eyes" (164). His is the regard which is to construct her, the gaze that comes the closest to being able to rescue her.

What, literally, does he see in Tess? Several times Tess appears as a spectacle presenting itself to the male gaze. The narrator himself seems to take delight in Tess's objectification, as in this scene in which she is caught in the glare of a train's headlight: "The light of the engine flashed for a second upon Tess Durbeyfield's figure, motionless under the great holly tree. No object could have looked more foreign to the gleaming cranks and wheels than this unsophisticated girl, with the round bare arms, the rainy face and hair, the suspended attitude of a friendly leopard at pause, the print gown of no date or fashion, and the cotton bonnet drooping on her brow" (269).

The sensual pleasure of this passage is derived from knowing Tess inside and out. Just as in the scene in which she was objectified as a fly, we have, until now, been very much inside Tess's consciousness, living with her at the dairy. We have experienced her doubts about her past and her present feelings for Angel. Now, for a flash, we are able to catch a glimpse of her as a train or a person from the city might catch her, frozen for an instant in our view, and then gone. The text relishes this disjuncture between the constituted objectivity and subjectivity of its heroine. Her "foreignness" and strangeness are emphasized in the bizarre comparison with a "friendly leopard." That defamiliarization, coupled with the familiar, even intimate, details of "round bare arms" and "rainy face and hair," give this scene its strangely powerful erotic air.

Angel's more personal views of Tess are no less eroticized or objectified. He watches her milking and observes that she makes a "picture," her profile against the cow as "keen as a cameo" (212): "The stillness of her head and features was remarkable: she might have been in a trance, her eyes open, yet unseeing. Nothing in the picture moved but Old Pretty's tail and Tess's pink hands, the latter so gently as to be a rhythmic pulsation only, as if they were obeying a reflex stimulus, like a beating heart" (212). This scene, as in the scene in which Tess is caught in the train's headlights, relies for its power on Tess being motionless and unseeing. She is caught, like an animal paralyzed by headlights, rendered completely visible, almost immobile, and blinded. She herself cannot see back.[15]

In this, as in so many other scenes, Angel's gaze focuses on her mouth: "To a young man with the least fire in him that little upward lift in the middle of her red top lip was distracting, infatuating, maddening. He had never before seen a woman's lips and teeth which forced upon his mind with such persistent iteration, the old Elizabethan simile of roses filled with snow" (212–13). In all these passages, the viewer is constructed as male, and even more particularly as a lusty heterosexual male. The phrase, "to a young man with the least fire in him" serves as challenge and incitement. As Boumelha notes, "The narrator's erotic fantasies of penetration and engulfment evoke an unusually overt maleness in the narrative voice" (120), thereby complicating other readers' relationship to character and text.

A second passage replicates and develops many of the issues presented here. Angel returns from a trip to find Tess in the dairy just waking up. Once again, the power of this passage, the impact of its spectacle (focused on Tess's mouth), depends for its effect on her own semi-conscious state, on her being unaware that she is watched: "She had not heard him enter, and hardly realized his presence there. She was yawning, and he saw the red interior of her mouth as if it had been a snake's. She had stretched one arm so high above her coiled-up cable of hair that he could see its satin delicacy above the sunburn; her face was flushed with sleep, and her eyelids hung heavy over their pupils. The brim-fulness of her nature breathed from her. It was a moment when a woman's soul is more incarnate than at any other time; when the most spiritual beauty bespeaks itself flesh; and sex takes the outside place in the presentation" (242-3).

The passage is remarkable for its sensual and particularized detail. Now Angel, and through him the reader, can see right into Tess. She is utterly particularized (fetishized) and distinguishable. Our privileged gaze reaches places usually left hidden, "the red interior of her mouth," "the satin delicacy" of her inner arm. The "brim-fulness of her nature," her "soul," and her "sex" are all on display here for Angel's and the reader's delectation. We all become voyeurs; unseen ourselves, we are granted almost limitless powers of visual penetration.

Just as in the other moments of visualization, moments when Tess was "lit up" by Angel's or the narrator's gaze, she herself is sightless. The attempt to distinguish and subjectify Tess, to rescue her from the oblivion of not being "an existence, an experience, a passion, a structure of sensations to anybody but herself," depends upon our being able to see and distinguish her. Based on the evidence of this scene, that attempt would – as far as it goes – appear to have succeeded. Tess is known and seen inside and out, but in the process has become fetishized, turned into an erotic object of desire. Without a gaze of her own, her subjectivity remains inert.

The problem with such an objectification or fetishization is that it requires an anaesthetized heroine. As Penny Boumelha notes of the scene in which Angel finds Tess yawning: "Here, as elsewhere, and particularly at moments of such erotic response, consciousness is all but edited out. Tess is asleep, or in reverie, at almost every crucial turn of the plot" (121).

We saw how Lovelace wanted to "try" or discover the nature of Clarissa's desire. His trial failed, however, because in drugging and raping her, he obliterated the very will and desire he sought. This is the danger in *Tess* as well. The life and eroticism of this novel depend upon our sense that Tess is *both* object and subject. The novel swings from one side of the dialectic to another. It claims to want to rescue Tess from objectivity and anonymity and attempts to do this through the obsession of its gaze. But if she is often "asleep or in reverie" when seen, her consciousness, as Boumelha puts it, is "edited out."

Tess's subjectivity appears, thus, to be little more than a chimera. The narrator implies that he wants the reader to feel her as "an existence, an experience, a passion, [and] a structure of sensations," but to do so would be to forfeit the erotic luxury of continually seeing her from the outside and then moving to her (imagined) interior.

Ellen Rooney has written that although "Hardy's novel is about the production of female subjectivity," it is a subjectivity that "exists here only in sexual difference."[16] She claims that if "[t]he masculine subject is the only subject of sexuality" (94), then "[a] feminine subject [such as Tess] who can act only to consent or refuse to consent is in fact denied subjectivity" (92). Tess's only role can be as the passive object of rape or seduction.[17] This appears to be yet another novel in which female subjectivity is produced only for the possession or enjoyment of the voyeuristic (heterosexual male) readerly gaze.

There is, however, *some* attempt to imagine female desire, some attempt to "feel as a woman" in Hardy's representation of Izzy, Marian and Retty, the three milkmaids at Talbothay's dairy. Desire, as they experience it, seems to be a part of the overall succulent fertility of the valley in summer: "Amid the oozing fatness and warm ferments of the Var Vale, at a season when the rush of juices could almost be heard below the hiss of fertilization, it was impossible that the most fanciful love should not grow passionate. The ready bosoms existing there were impregnated by their surroundings" (210). Tess and Angel are not the only ones touched by the "hiss of fertilization." "The oozing fatness and warm ferments" form the element in which all of them live, breathe, and work. All are equally "impregnated by their surroundings." Female desire as represented in this novel spills over like milk. Once created (and this text is, I think, nearly unique in mainstream English fiction for attempting to represent female sexual desire), there seems to be a surplus. Feelings, once aroused, are difficult to suppress, are "catching." We are warned that "there is contagion in this sentiment, especially among women" (206). The women lie in their hot attic room during the summer nights, burning with love for Angel: "The air of the

sleeping-chamber seemed to palpitate with the hopeless passion of
the girls. They writhed feverishly under the oppressiveness of an
emotion thrust on them by cruel Nature's law" (207). Desire, as it
is experienced by women, does not appear to impel them forward,
or stimulate them to bold and heroic action as it does men. Instead,
it leaves them lying panting, tossing, and turning beneath the eaves.
Held in "cruel Nature's" grip, they again become objects of pity.

When Angel Clare saw the girls on the green dancing without
partners, he was impelled to help them out: "'This is a thousand
pities,' he said gallantly ... 'Where are your partners, my dears?'"
(25). In this text female desire seems to have been created to give
the hero a place and a rationale. They waited on the green and they
wait to be helped across the stream. They all wait to love him. They
are helpless awaiting his rescue. They have been overwhelmed,
felled by a force larger than themselves. The force of this overwhelming passion threatens once again to obliterate Tess's identity:
"The differences which distinguished them as individuals were
abstracted by this passion and each was but portion of one organ-
ism called sex" (207-8). In a similar fashion, when the four girls
had waited for Angel to carry them across the stream, their "four
hearts gave a big throb simultaneously" (201). However hard text
and reader work to distinguish Tess, and bring her up out of the
background, she appears doomed to recede once again. It is ironic
that the very construction of her desire which might have differentiated, individualized, or subjectified her, serves merely to inscribe
her once again into sameness.

Angel's first enunciation of "a thousand pities" is not the last.
The statement is uttered at least two more times – by women. As
Tess sits nursing her sick and illegitimate child, Sorrow, in the field,
one of the other fieldworkers comments on Tess's bad luck at being
distinguished by fate in such a way: "'twas a thousand pities that it
should have happened to she, of all others. But 'tis always the
comeliest!" (27). The narrator continues: "It was a thousand pities,
indeed; it was impossible for even an enemy to feel otherwise on
looking at Tess as she sat there, with her flower-like mouth and
large tender eyes .... an almost standard woman, but for the slight
incautiousness of character inherited from her race" (127–8). The
fieldwoman hints that more than fate was at work in marking Tess.
Her "comeliness" marked her first. The narrator develops this, and
takes it in a slightly different direction by stressing that what dis-

tinguishes Tess, what makes her *not* just a "standard woman," is something other than her beauty; it is her "slight incautiousness of character." The point is that she is marked both by beauty *and* by her defect (the nature of which is never entirely clear). Ever so delicately, in a remark that merely glances off the page, the narrator hints at Tess's responsibility for her fate. Because they are so inextricably linked, it is almost impossible to sort out which comes first – Tess's beauty or her pain. Does her beauty cause her pain,[18] or does the pain make her more attractive?

J. Hillis Miller was right in noting that no "single accounting cause" can be found for Tess's suffering (141). While there may not be a readily apparent *cause*, there seems to be at the very least a metonymic relation between Tess's sexuality and her pain. One is insistently linked to the other. Just as Angel is attracted by and finally able to distinguish Tess on the green by his sense that she has been hurt by him, so we readers are similarly implicated into feelings of guilt and sympathy. Angel feels he has hurt Tess by not noticing her; others (like Alec) hurt her by noticing her. In either case she is hurt and all that we can offer is our pity.

Men and women alike are drawn to pity Tess. The phrase "a thousand pities" is offered up for the third time when the milkmaid, Izzy, sees Tess alone and abandoned by her husband:" ''Tis a thousand pities your husband can't see 'ee now – you do look a real beauty!' said Izz Huett ... Izz spoke with a magnanimous abandonment of herself to the situation: she could not be – no woman with a heart bigger than a hazel-nut could be – antagonistic to Tess in her presence, the influence which she exercised over those of her own sex being of a warmth and strength quite unusual" (407). Any "woman with a heart bigger than a hazel-nut" is going to feel for Tess. But the pity represented here felt by one woman for another is impotent, can only wish that Tess might be seen – seen compassionately, seen for her beauty and seen as Izz sees her – *by a man*. Izzy's wish for Tess is the classic female wish for a male rescuer. She herself can do nothing, can imagine no other way to help. This is Tess's tragedy: "The eye returns involuntarily to [her]." She cannot escape our gaze, and our gaze, helplessly, connects us to her in an unending and vicious cycle of pity and lust. The ending is unbearable because we are all caught in a relationship we cannot escape.

6 "Back Talk" – The Work of Margaret Atwood and Angela Carter

For one moment, just one moment, Fevvers suffered the worst crisis of her life: "Am I fact? Or am I fiction?"
                                                                Angela Carter[1]

It's all very well to say I refuse to be a victim, but then you have to look at the context in which one is or isn't a victim. You can't simply refuse. You can refuse to define yourself that way, but it's not quite so simple as that.
                                                                Margaret Atwood[2]

"Am I fact or am I fiction?" wonders Fevvers, the heroine of Angela Carter's *Nights at the Circus*. "Am I what I think I am?" she continues. "Or am I what he thinks I am?" (290). Such questions, causing Fevvers to suffer "the worst crisis of her life," are central to the theme of these two final chapters. In this chapter, I turn to the work of two highly conscious and articulate female writers of the twentieth century in order to interrogate with them the literary heritage from and against which they write. In their own fiction they seek to re-discover and re-define female identity, which has itself in large part been constructed through fiction.

There is a sense in which the work of both Margaret Atwood and Angela Carter "talks back" to the literary tradition from which it springs, a sense in which their work probes and questions the status of the heroine in the novel and in society.[3] But this work is equally concerned with the future; whether they present utopias, dystopias, or something in between, these authors seek ways out of the here and now. Theirs are highly conscious and sophisticated viewpoints, alert to the dangers and powers of fictional representation. One of the problems involved in talking back to such a tradition is the extent to which that very tradition itself has defined woman as "other," as the object of speech and of desire, and as the passive heroine needing rescue. I see the work of Atwood and Carter as representative of the attempt by women to claim subjectivity for themselves, to represent women as *subjects* of speech and of desire, as rescuers rather than victims.[4] These are not easy tasks.

The difficulty becomes apparent as soon as we speak of talking back, for how does one talk back to a tradition which has defined one as other, which has raised doubts about the nature of one's own identity and one's own ability to speak? Is it any wonder, then, that some of the first assertions from these writers should be questions and expressions of puzzlement about their status and their identity? "Am I fact or am I fiction," they ask. Do I trust what I think I know, or believe what *he* thinks he knows about me? The questions are valid, for how *can* women know what they are "really" like when it is fiction that has defined that reality?

A logical first step might seem to be to deny the representations and roles of the past, to look at them and say, "This is not me, this is not mine," but Margaret Atwood and Angela Carter are writers in a postmodern era in which one has learned to take the reality of fiction seriously. As they are aware, fiction has shaped our reality to such a large extent that it has become hard to locate any reality that might exist entirely outside of fiction. The two seem virtually inseparable. The real questions these authors face are: what kind of fiction will *they* themselves write? How will their own personal realities shape that fiction? And finally, what kind of reality will their fiction in turn produce?

The logical *first* step may be to try to deny the representations and roles of the past. But after denial, what? It may be all very well, Margaret Atwood reminds us in the epigraph above, "To say [like the narrator of *Surfacing*] I refuse to be a victim, but ... you can't simply refuse. You can refuse to define yourself that way, but it's not quite so simple as that." Her words are, at one and the same time, adamant and tentative, defiant and uncertain. One *can* refuse (surely one *must* refuse) to be defined as a victim, and yet the weight of at least 250 years of tradition (*Clarissa* was published in

1747) is such that it is hard to try now to begin to imagine radically new roles and new ways of being. After two or three centuries how does one see oneself if *not* as a victim? And even if, individually, we are able to shrug off this role, are we not bound to recognize its social reality, the reality of women who are forced to live now as victims in our society? Far from excluding the representations of the past, Atwood and Carter's novels are *saturated* with the language and attitudes of times past. *Handmaid's Tale* is a futuristic reworking of *The Scarlet Letter* and similar works. Carter's actual language, her words, phrases, and sentences, are filled with references to Shakespeare, Yeats, Joyce, Swift, and others. These writers look to the past in order to imagine the future. As Atwood writes about Carter, "To combat traditional myths about the nature of woman, she constructs other, more subversive ones" ("Running with Tigers" 122).

In earlier chapters I considered *Clarissa*, *Scarlet Letter*, *Portrait*, and *Tess* each as a type of school of sympathy and identification, as a place where one might learn both to feel *for* and to feel *as* a woman. In each novel the heroine's suffering serves as a catalyst for the reader's emotional involvement and aesthetic pleasure. Out of her pain comes our pity. Reading these novels teaches us to feel for her and moves us to attempt to feel as she feels. But ours is an identification that is predicated on distance, division, and difference.

Foremost among the differences created in these novels is sexual difference. Those characters who watch the heroine and feel most strongly for her are primarily (though not exclusively) male (Belford, Morden, and Lovelace in *Clarissa*, Chillingworth and Dimmesdale in *The Scarlet Letter*, Ralph Touchett, Caspar Goodwood, and Lord Warburton in *The Portrait of a Lady*, Alec d'Urberville and Angel Clare in *Tess of the d'Urbervilles*). In each novel, the reader's identification with the heroine is thus routed through male characters. It seems likely that identification *depends* upon difference, giving male characters, because of their distance and difference from the heroine, the advantage of being able to form sympathetic attachments to her. This would mean that the production of identification and sympathy depends upon the reader's distance and difference from the position of the heroine. It is perhaps to guarantee this distance and this difference that our reading positions are constructed as masculine. We can only feel for the heroine, that is feel for her as the text would have it, to the extent

that we are distanced from her. This means that the reader needs to
read as a man in order to *feel* "as a woman." Our identification is
built out of a type of sympathy which in turn depends upon distance. Woman reading as man in order to feel as woman becomes
a complex ritual of cross-dressing wherein gender roles are strictly
defined only to be transgressed and borders are set only to be
crossed.

The search for the mystery of female desire is closely linked to
questions of female voice and female action or heroism. The heroine's voice and her actions are contingent upon her desire. I will be
considering Atwood's *Surfacing* and *The Handmaid's Tale*, and
Carter's *The Bloody Chamber* and *Nights at the Circus* as works
which begin, not to *answer* these questions, but only to *consider*
them. I approach these works by way of three interrelated topoi:
Desire, Voice, and Action/Rescue/Heroism.

DESIRE

The early novels, *Clarissa*, *The Scarlet Letter*, *Portrait of a Lady*,
and *Tess of the d'Urbervilles*, have been discussed as attempts to
feel as a woman, to try to imagine what a woman might feel. Such
attempts, predicated on distance and indirection, meant that the
reader's experience of the heroine's desire is *never* direct, *never*
unmediated. It is always experienced from at least one remove. It
can be argued that it is just this shade of difference that creates our
experience of desire in novels. For it seems that desire is constructed out of the split in each novel between the adoring and sympathizing male narrator/hero/reader and the suffering innocent heroine. Does *all* desire depend upon the desire of another? Luce Irigaray wrote that woman participates in "a desire that is not her
own" (*This Sex* 25) and was interested in discovering a female
desire that might exist outside of, or separate from, male desire, but
we have to wonder whether *any* desire, male or female, can exist so
autonomously.

This, in part, was René Girard's argument in *Deceit, Desire and
the Novel*, in which he proposed a triangular model of desire. In
this model, the desire of one male is awakened not by the woman
in and of herself, but by another man's desire for her. (Eve Kosofsky Sedgwick uses Girard's insight as a springboard for her own

analysis of homo-social relations in *Between Men*.[5]) Girard's analysis was ground breaking in its demonstration that desire was neither simple nor single, that it was an affair involving more than two. According to his model, desire is produced from the spectacle of (what we take to be) another's desire.

Similarly, our desire as readers is constructed out of the various desires represented in the text. What we feel in the four early novels – for Clarissa, Hester, Isabel, and Tess – is not so much for the heroine herself, as it is for the mystery of her own desire (which in these novels is a desire for death and punishment). Therefore, our own desire (constructed as masculine) to have, possess, or collect the heroine becomes intertwined with and eventually virtually indistinguishable from her own desire for self-destruction.[6]

If desire is itself, in its essence, built out of a split, structured around the desire of the other, then any attempt by a twentieth-century postmodern feminist writer to re-create, re-appropriate or rediscover some unsullied female desire will be impossible. It may be that we all, all the time, participate in a desire that is not our own. It may be that there is no other kind of desire, that "not our own" is its fundamental constituent.[7]

VOICE

Otherness is as important in the construction of voice as it is in the construction of desire. Each is similarly organized around division or difference. Just as one relies on another's desire to create a desire of one's own (we are moved by the desire of a man for a woman, the desire of a woman for pain), so one cannot speak without using the language and the voice of the other. Woman has traditionally served as the "other" around which these were constructed, the difference from which desire and sometimes voice could spring. If she is to be the subject, what will change?

I argued earlier that the form of the novel seemed inextricably bound with the representation and construction of desire, and that that desire was always built from or built around the desire of another. It seems just as true to say that the novel is constructed around and through the *voice* of another. This, of course, is Mikhail Bakhtin's argument. He claims that the novel is, in its very essence, dialogic, depending for its existence upon the inclusion of the voice from outside which mocks and contradicts: "The image of another's language and outlook on the world, simultaneously represented and representing is," he writes, "extremely typical of the novel"(*Dialogic Imagination* 45).

In *Problems of Dostoevsky's Poetics*, Bakhtin discusses Dostoevsky's "polyphonic" novel, made up of voices which not only talk to each other, but are in themselves doubled and dialogic: "In every voice [Dostoevsky] could hear two contending voices, in every expression a crack" (30). Bakhtin's insistence on dialogism is an insistence on something more than mere dialogue. It involves not just a question of two monadic and indivisible entities in conversation, but a sense that every voice or word is itself already divided, already permeated with the language of the other: "When a member of a speaking collective comes upon a word, it is not as a neutral word of language, not as a word free from the aspirations and evaluations of others, uninhabited by others' voices. No, he receives the word from another's voice and filled with that other voice. The word enters his context from another context, permeated with the interpretations of others. His own thought finds the word already inhabited" (202). Women have learned this lesson well; they already know that their language is filled with the tracks and the traces of the other.[8] To some extent these earlier novels have reversed that situation; it is the specter of the woman's voice and presence which lingers in the male author's words.

Of the novels I have looked at so far, in only *Clarissa* does the heroine appear to speak "directly." The epistolary style of that novel allows us privileged and intimate access to Clarissa's thoughts and voice. The other novels, narrated by what we assume is a male narrator, approach their heroines less directly and offer us less privileged access to her. But all four novels are characterized by a vacillation between intimacy and closeness – moments in which we know the heroine, think her thoughts, see what she sees, and feel what she feels – and moments of distance in which the heroine is objectified, seen from afar, and made distant and strange. Even in *Clarissa*, where we do hear some of the story in her own words, her tale is repeatedly contradicted, overridden, and swallowed up by the accounts of others. As she fades and dies, her story comes to be narrated almost entirely by her executor, Belford, who presents her papers (and thus frames her voice). He speaks, but his voice is filled with the voice of Clarissa. His voice contains hers. ("His own thought finds the word already inhabited.") Her voice, then, like her desire, is productive, but used always at a remove, from a distance.

Neither desire nor voice appears to be the pure monadic entity we once took it for. Instead each seems to be built upon and generated out of gaps and splits, division and difference.

ACTION/RESCUE/HEROISM

The third of the points under consideration is the possibilty of female heroic action. If a woman is to assume full subjectivity, she must know what it is that she wants and know how to speak that desire. Only then might she be able to act on it. Each of the heroines of the earlier novels is characterized by her inability to act or to free herself from the circumstances which entangle and engulf her. Helpless and imprisoned, she is unable to act for herself, though others are profoundly moved by her state. Her helplessness and lack of power in one area grant her a new power, the power of seduction. Readers are seduced. We are moved by her plight and stirred to sympathy and identification. This response of ours is generated by what I call the rescue narrative, a narrative type almost archetypal in our culture.

The rescue narrative has many versions, the simplest of which can be signalled by the words "damsel in distress" or "knight in shining armour." The woman (Sleeping Beauty, Snow White) lies helpless and motionless. She waits for the prince, the knight, to rescue and to free her. This is a potent myth in our culture and one with clear and rigid gender stereotypes. It forms the basis of countless fairy tales and is the myth which Georges Poulet invokes when he describes the effect of seeing books lying helpless in a bookshop: "They wait for someone to come and deliver them from their materiality, from their immobility ... Are they aware that an act of man might suddenly transform their existence? ... I find it hard to resist their appeal" (53). This myth offers only two roles or subject positions; active male or passive female, hero or victim. Although these roles are utterly distinct, Poulet's account would seem to indicate that they are, nevertheless, interdependent. In his account, his subjectivity (here, virtually indistinguishable from his masculinity) is roused, stirred, even brought into being by the books' abject objectness ("they wait for someone to come and deliver them from their materiality, from their immobility"). It is his sense of their arrested or frozen plenitude that stirs him to action. His heroic posture, his masculine response, is roused by the spectacle of books which (while never explicitly stated as such) are patently feminized in their passivity and seductiveness.

The hero position, Teresa de Lauretis tells us, is masculine: "Man is by definition the subject of culture and of any social act" ("Violence" 250). She argues persuasively that the actant role in narrative is masculine, that even when a woman assumes this role, she does so not as a woman but as a man. Such is the regulatory force of narrative. My first claim, therefore, is that the spectacle of suffering woman rouses the hero-subject (by definition masculine) into being. To the extent that we are outraged by the unfairness of the treatment these heroines receive, to the extent that we feel roused to righteous anger and want to rescue her, we are all, male and female alike, "masculinized," that is, subjectified and empowered. This would seem to be borne out by other characters' responses to the heroine within the novels. As mentioned above, most of those who love and appreciate the heroines are male. Many of them seek to rescue her and/or seek revenge on her behalf. Cousin Morden, Belford, Ralph, Casper Goodwood, Alec and Angel: all seek in various ways to rescue the heroine.

Even when a character is female, as rescuer she is masculinized. Both Anna Howe in *Clarissa* and Henrietta Stackpole in *Portrait of a Lady* feel outrage and pity for their friends. But they are portrayed as mannish which makes them somewhat ridiculous in the eyes of the text. They cannot be taken as seriously as a Ralph or a Belford so they become, to some extent, comic figures (this is more true of Henrietta than of Anna). Because they are defined by their seemingly unique independence, and will be hard for any man to subdue, marriage is viewed as something of a wonder and something of a joke.[9] To the extent that they are caricatures, their ability to help or rescue their friends is curtailed; they are denied full hero-positions.

In the forest scene in *The Scarlet Letter*, it is Hester Prynne who acts as potential rescuer. There is no comedy in her assumption of the role. Instead, she is magnificent. Charismatic and forceful, she urges Dimmesdale (who has become passive to the point of becoming masochistic and thus feminized) to rouse himself and to escape with her. But the more she is roused to action the more feminized Dimmesdale becomes. Society and her role as mother (it is Pearl who tells her to put the A back on) check her heroic potential.[10]

None of our heroines is able to save herself, but in *The Portrait of a Lady* Isabel does attempt some heroic action on the behalf of another. As many have noted, the plight of Pansy, Isabel's stepdaughter, is a mirror of her own. Pansy serves as a more subservient version of herself. Pansy is *literally* locked up, put into the convent which Isabel recognizes as "a well-appointed prison" (456), a "great penal establishment" (460). But unlike Isabel, Pansy offers no resistance and refuses to fight back. She "bowed her pretty head to authority and only asked of authority to be merciful" (462). Isabel is moved by Pansy's plight, and while realizing that there is little she can do for her, does promise that she will not desert her (462). Ever so tentatively, Isabel is putting herself into the position of hero/rescuer. The irony of course is that by assuming such a role, she becomes a kind of martyr, assuring her own victimization and closing off all avenues for her own escape.

It seems that in every case the rescue fantasy that these novels present is compounded by a simultaneous narrative, a narrative that weakens, complicates, and in many cases subverts the first, operating as a kind of thanatos to its eros. This is the death wish within the rush toward life, love, and safety, a wish manifested in the sense of helplessness these novels create.[11] If, on the one hand, we are empowered and masculinized by the spectacle of female victimization (roused to righteous indignation and heroic action), on the other hand we are also infected with a lassitude, a sense of helplessness almost feminine in its powerlessness. The would-be male rescuers in the novels – Belford and Morden, Ralph, Caspar Goodwood and Lord Warburton, and Angel Clare – in spite of their sympathy and good intentions, are all, without exception, ineffectual. Their heroic efforts are, in Tess's words, "too late." And the reader, like these hapless heroes, is first roused by the spectacle of female victimization to a state of full and heroic subjectivity only to be "infected" by the hopelessness, the passivity, and the decline of the heroine. This narrative thread disempowers as the first empowers. If we think of these novels as social agents doing social work, then the work of the second narrative thread is to disempower subjects, allowing them to feel "full" of emotion but void of ambition or the will to change. The drive to rescue and the urge to give up are, I believe, equally strong and equally present in all the novels considered here.

To feel oneself as a rescuer is to feel empowered, energetic, full of power and potency, but it is not at all clear that this is the feeling we are left with in *The Portrait* or any of the other three novels. In another very real sense what we actually seem to experience is a diminution of our own range, a weakening of our powers. When Richard Poirier writes of *The Portrait of a Lady* that "there can be no such thing as the 'freedom' which Isabel wants ... simply for the reason that ... there are in everyone the flaws, the fears, the neuroses that fix and confine and stifle" (207), his point is that James is simply identifying and describing pre-existent fears and neuroses that fix, confine and stifle all of us. My point is that novels, such as *The Portrait* may have something to do with transmitting and creating those fears. These novels teach us the readers – through the pleasure of identification with the female victim – to accommodate ourselves to discipline, denial, and repression. As Foucault puts it in *Discipline and Punish*, "Everyone must see punishment not only as natural, but in his own interest" (109). Discipline becomes a form of pain we all must learn.

Novels like this teach us several lessons. First: there is power to be gained from passivity. This is feminine power (as it has been defined in our culture, the only power readily accorded to women), the power to lure or seduce the gaze and the attention of the other. This lesson infects or undercuts the other message, which is that – having been moved by the plight of these victims – we could do anything about it. The two narrative patterns operate by granting two types of power, the power of the rescuer and the power of the victim. There is pleasure to be had and power to be gained from *both* positions, beautiful helpless maiden *and* brave and fearless rescuer. I am arguing that the reader is invited to participate in or to "try out" both roles. It is not at all clear that as readers of these novels we simply gain voyeuristic/sadistic pleasure out of watching another suffer while we ourselves remain free.[12] Some of the pleasure we take is from imagining ourselves victims, imagining ourselves being watched and pitied.[13]

It may be almost impossible to narrate a story of rescue without, at the very least, invoking the rigidly gendered stereotypes on which it seems to depend. As we will see, particularly in Carter's work, these stereotypes can be invoked only to be overturned. To the extent that we feel helpless and await rescue, we feel "feminine." To the extent that we are "pricked up," feel outrage, and are moved to act, we feel "masculine." We experience the power inherent in each of these positions through gender. But I argue that the novels allow all of us, male and female, to experience both. As we shall see, these are narrative patterns and stereotypes which Carter and Atwood explore and test.

The four earlier novels depended on a type of dialogism, an imagined representation of what the feminine might be, what a woman might see, what she might think, want, and feel. Out of and from this othernesss were spun desire, voice, and the narrative of heroic action. In these works the gap was explicitly gendered; they depended upon woman's assuming the place of other. Male authors, narrators, and characters atttempted to feel through their female heroines. In turning to twentieth-century works by female authors, I am trying to discover whether the constitutive gaps that we saw in the earlier novels are erased or whether they remain, and if so, in what ways. In the earlier novels there was always a sense of distance, a gap to be bridged between narrator and heroine and between reader and heroine. This was the gap out of which sympathy and identification were forged. In all these twentieth-century fictions, narrated often in the first person by female narrators, the gap remains. Feeling *as* a subject, feeling *as* a woman is no less problematic; the situation is no less alienated. The split, the gap, the distance, remains.

I turn now to Margaret Atwood and Angela Carter, two authors who deal with the history of female representation and who self-consciously try to assess what that tradition means for them as women and as novelists. Their fiction works to rethink woman as heroine and subject, and to consider what a new possession of subjectivity might mean for woman's voice and desire. The two authors approach the problem differently, but neither represents woman as effortlessly assuming full voice, full desire, or full heroism. As Atwood says in her interview, "It's not so simple as that."

BORDERS

It seems fitting that this work on identification and difference should conclude with a study of two female novelists who are obsessed with the idea of borders. The concept of border or boundary – important in all four of the works considered in this chapter – is most central in Margaret Atwoood's *Surfacing*.

Borders are the lines by which we mark identity and difference. Everything on this side of the line, we say, is one, a coherent and indivisible whole. Everything on the other side is alien and strange, is, in short, *other*. Gradations and ruptures, differences within or similarities between: these ideas complicate and confuse the clear precision and logic of our borderlines. We use borders and boundaries to help keep things straight, to name and identify, to mark differences.

Just as female is defined in opposition to male, we set off other terms, one against the other, in order to understand them: past vs present, present vs future, human vs animal, culture vs nature, primitive vs civilized. My list is taken from just some of the binarisms Atwood and Carter explore and challenge in their fiction. Theirs is fiction about borders, threshholds, and frontiers, about no man's lands. No limit is left untested; nothing is taken for granted. Even the most basic distinctions, such as those dividing human from animal or past from present, are questioned. Pridefully and ironically perverse, the authors play with notions of identity and difference, and in the process, rethink the heroine's ability to want, to speak, and to act.

Atwood and Carter realize that, while one may not be able to simply deny or refuse the identity that a border has constructed, one *can* play with and question its limits. Our difference from animals may not be of the type we had always assumed. Similarly it may be that we are living in the future now, or that the past is not so distant as we think. Woman may have to take on the role of victim in order to break it apart and re-emerge as hero. All these possibilities are examined in the fiction of Angela Carter and Margaret Atwood.

Their explorations in these areas are evidence of their interest in what the anthropologist, Victor Turner, has called liminality. He explains it this way: "The attributes of liminality or of liminal *personae* ('threshhold people') are necessarily ambiguous, since this condition and these persons elude or slip through the network of classifications that normally locate states and positions in cultural space"(95). The liminal is that which challenges and ruptures the borderlines of classification on which society depends. It is that which exists between or across borders.

Liminality is also part of a rite of passage, a time of change. The liminal, then, is of use to the feminist writer in that she need not adhere to traditional classifications; her ideas and characters can be "ambiguous," can "slip through" old networks by using conventional terms in an unconventional way. The liminal is also useful because, as an element in rites of passage, it allows the writer to imagine something new.

There are also similarities, it seems to me, between Turner's "liminality" and Bakhtin's notion of heteroglossia. Turner writes that "what is interesting about liminal phenomena ... is the blend they offer of lowliness and sacredness" (96). This is reminiscent of Bakhtin's insight into the way parody mocks and travesties the monologic in novels. Bakhtin would say that Turner's liminality, the inclusion of the high and the low, the sacred and the profane, is "extremely typical" of novels.

If this blend, this "liminality," is "extremely typical" of the novel, then Atwood and Carter can be viewed as both traditional *and* radical, for the traditional novel, at least according to Bakhtin, has always been iconoclastic.[14] The tradition calls for borders to be challenged and the monologic to be disrupted by the inclusion of the voice of the other. The dialogic, the inclusion of two voices, two differing points of view, is essential to the construction of the novel. As Bakhtin puts it, "One language can, after all, see itself only in light of another language" (*Dialogic Imagination*, 12). Otherness is, as it were, written into the script.

MARGARET ATWOOD

Surfacing

The unnamed narrator of Margaret Atwood's *Surfacing* is a heroine in search of her place in the world. The place she hopes to find is pure and uncontaminated, untouched by the ruin and devastation she sees around her. Those who ruin, those who contaminate and kill are defined variously as men, as Americans, and finally, as human.[15] Those who are passive, innocent, and therefore victims, the other half of the binarisms, are women, Canadians, and animals.

The place of purity that the narrator seeks is never found; mirage-like, its image beckons only to disappear when one approaches. As she drives north with three friends, she notices evidence of encroaching ruin. The opening words of the novel set the tone, establishing her numbed paranoid state: "I can't believe I'm on this road again, twisting along past the lake where the white birches are dying, the disease is spreading up from the south" (7). In her eyes the journey is a frantic and probably doomed rush to escape the disease spreading up from the south. They are heading, in her friend David's words, to "the true north strong and free" (13). These words, it would appear, can only be said, now at the end of the twentieth century, with irony and some bitterness. Truth? Strength? Freedom? We doubt it. But the mirage lingers; the illusion persists. However much she doubts, the narrator is nonetheless drawn to a place which, if not the true north strong and free, can at least be defined by what it is *not*. (It is not polluted, not American.) What it is, what it might be, continues to elude her.

After crossing the border, she says, "Now we're on my home ground, foreign territory" (11). She reaches "home" only to find it "foreign" in several senses. It is foreign to herself and her friends because, we can assume, they have been immersed in American culture. It is also foreign in that American culture is so powerful and subsuming that the people who live in the region see themselves as "different," feel foreign even when they're at home.[16] And finally, it is foreign to the narrator in that it *never* was hers. She and her family were Anglo-Protestants living in a French-Catholic region. When she stops in the town to shop, her accent, her clothes, her unmarried status mark her as an outsider, as alien. When she thinks back to the past, she realizes that she had never belonged: "But the truth is that I don't know what the villagers thought about, I was so shut off from them. The older ones occasionally crossed themselves when we passed, possibly because my mother was wearing slacks, but even that was never explained. Although we played during visits with the solemn, slightly hostile children of Paul and Madame, the games were brief and wordless" (54).

The only way that the village can appear familiar or look like home is when the narrator has gained some distance from it, has achieved some perspective. Leaving the village to go up the lake in search of her father, she re-assesses it: "I wait until we're in the middle of the lake. At the right moment I look over my shoulder as I always did and there is the village, suddenly distanced and clear, the houses receding and grouping, the white church startling against the dark of the trees. The feeling I expected before but failed to have comes now, homesickness, for a place where I never lived, I'm far enough away" (30–1). She feels homesickness for a place in which she's never lived, a place in which she's never felt at home. The feeling comes from distance, when she's "far enough away."

However misguided her quest, it is driven by a need that is real, a need to heal the split, feel less cut off, to find a home in which to feel whole: "I'd allowed myself to be cut in two ... there had been an accident and I came apart. The other half, the one locked away, was the only one that could live; I was the wrong half, detached, terminal. I was nothing but a head, or no, something minor like a severed thumb; numb" (108). She attempts to find that home, the place where she can feel whole again, in nature or in the past, somewhere away from human beings and the "disease" around her. Her search for the "other side," away from what she sees as the devastation and ruin wrought by Americans, men, and humans, leads her further and further away from the u.s., from civilization, and eventually, away from language and logic itself. The novel is the story of how and why such a search is both necessary and doomed.

This move toward purity and integrity necessitates strict borders, high fences, and strong gates. The narrator is not quite sure what she is looking for, but she is sure of what she wants to avoid. Her friend David puts it this way: "It wouldn't be a bad country if only we could kick out the fucking pig Americans, eh? Then we could have some peace" (89). These thoughts echo the narrator's own, but, as she slowly comes to realize, this view is not only naive but self-destructive because, while filling her with rage and bitterness, it does nothing to empower her. On the contrary, it leaves her weak, a victim. The problem with an attitude like the narrator's or David's is that it relies so exclusively on limits and borders. The narrator's strong sense of "us versus them" means that she accords to "them" all power and thus all subjectivity, seeing herself as only an object. She abdicates her own responsibilities and powers as a subject.

Without a will and a gaze of her own, she becomes, in her own mind at least, little more than a target for the aggression and the gaze of others. "Binoculars trained on me, I could feel the eye rays, cross of the rifle sight on my forehead, in case I made a false move" (118). Thoroughly victimized, she has come to the point at which fear is her predominant emotion, her only sensation: "I rehearsed emotions, naming them: joy, peace, guilt, release, love and hate, react, relate; what to feel was like what to wear, you watched the others and memorized it. But the only thing there was the fear that I wasn't alive" (111). What she *can* feel are the imagined "eye rays" of the enemy, trained on her forehead, ready to shoot. It is in response to this fear, this overwhelming sense of total victimization, that the narrator seeks to escape.[17] She seeks a place without borders and enemies, a place where the battles of man vs woman, American vs Canadian, culture vs nature, are not waged, a place from which she can learn to feel, to speak and to act. In other words, she seeks a place from which she can reclaim her subjectivity.

She is not only cut off from her own emotions – "I realized I didn't feel much of anything, I hadn't for a long time" (105) – but she also feels alienated and distanced from both her language and her voice: "It was the language again. I couldn't use it because it wasn't mine ... I hunted through my brain for any emotion that would coincide with what I'd said ... 'I'm trying to tell the truth,' I said. The voice wasn't mine, it came from someone dressed as me, imitating me" (106–7). Because she does not know what she feels, because she cannot trust her language or her voice to speak for her, this woman cannot yet become either subject or heroine. She feels that in order to find her own feelings and voice she has to retreat before she can advance, that she needs to retreat behind strict borders and needs to erect strong gates around herself. And indeed she does turn away from established culture, logic and language in order to find herself. "First I had to immerse myself in the other language" (158).

This quest for wholeness and identity leads the narrator to descend into a realm where borderlines – distinctions between past and present, animal amd human, primitive and civilized – are blurred or even erased. She chooses to retreat from all of those she has identified as the enemy: "But then I realized it wasn't the men I hated, it was the Americans, the human beings, men and women both. They'd had their chance but they had turned against the gods, and it was time for me to choose sides" (154). She has chosen sides, moved to one side of the borderline, and closed the door. When the narrator's friend Anna exclaims, "God, she really is inhuman" (154), she fails to realize the true insight and prophecy of her own remark.

At the beginning of the novel, the narrator enters "border country" (26), but by the end she finds herself in the place of the gods or spirits in which there is "an absence of defining borders" (83). The spirits, she finds, do not like fences, are "against borders": "Now I understand the rule. They can't be anywhere that's marked out, enclosed: even if I opened the doors and fences they could not pass in, to houses and cages, they can move only in the spaces between them, they are against borders" (180).

Her descent into the underworld, although driven by the passive fear of the victim, turns paradoxically into a very tentative type of heroism. Her descent into the place without borders allows her at least to *consider* a return to the realm of borders. When she returns from her sojourn in the spirit world, she begins to make herself ready to enter the world of houses, enclosures, and borders. For the narrator, coming back to language and culture involves an admission of guilt and relinquishment of the position of innocent victim: "This above all, to refuse to be a victim. Unless I can do that I can do nothing. I have to recant, give up the old belief that I am powerless and because of it nothing I can do will ever hurt anyone ... withdrawing is no longer possible and the alternative is death" (191).

The transition from victim to heroine is *not*, however, so simple as a critic such as Annis Pratt would have it: "She thus transforms herself from victim to hero, turning patriarchal space inside out so that it can no longer limit her being. Although the reader does not experience the hero's return to society, her impression is that she can never be returned to a peripheral or secondary status" (156). Sherrill Grace's account would seem to be more accurate. While Pratt sees the narrator's transformation as a simple one which, once completed can never be re-done, Grace sees a complex pattern of recurring descent and ascent. Grace, by pointing to Atwood's employment of the Persephone myth, allows us another, more complex, reading: "The descent-ascent pattern follows the paradigm of the Persephone myth, a myth Atwood has found attractive from her earliest poetry on. The narrator, a Persephone figure, must not only experience the underworld before returning to her Mother, but her descent also leads to the knowledge that she must henceforth embody *both* worlds; never again can she inhabit one or the other" (*Violent Duality* 105). The title of Atwood's novel is *Surfacing*, but it is as much about diving, as much about going down as it is about coming back up.[18] Following the Persephone myth, we cannot expect the narrator's transformation to be complete and unchangeable. Winter must follow summer so that summer can come again. Borders exist between life and death, madness and sanity, culture and nature, but perhaps they can be crossed and recrossed.

The novel ends with the narrator not crossing anything, "*yet.*" She stands poised, although whether to dive or to surface, is not quite clear. Undecided, she teeters between two worlds: "I tense forward, towards the demands and questions, though my feet do not move yet" (192).[19] Part 1 ended with a similar balancing act. There she stood half in and half out of the lake "till finally being in the air is more painful than being in the water and I bend and push myself reluctantly into the lake" (75).

Although the novel offers us no simple answers and gives us no clear direction, it does portray a heroine fighting to regain power, wanting to learn to live with and use power as wisely and as reasonably as possible without being crushed by it. She is a heroine exploring the borderline between victimization and heroism.[20] She gropes toward a sense of her own desire and voice, still untested and unknown. The novel, thus, offers a hopeful, though far from simplistic, outlook on the possibility of female heroism and subjectivity, a hope which seems to fade in Atwood's later work.

The Handmaid's Tale

Like Atwood's earlier *Surfacing*, *The Handmaid's Tale* is driven by paranoia, fueled by the victim's edgy unease. But if *Surfacing* was an exploration of a possible way out of victimization, *The Handmaid's Tale* is the story of what victimization feels like from the inside. This time there would appear to be no exit. In *Surfacing*, the narrator had to descend into a kind of primitive essentialism in her quest for power, integrity, and feminine subjectivity. In *The Handmaid's Tale* Offred, while more totally imprisoned than that narrator, has the fully developed desire and voice she never achieved. What Offred lacks, however, is the ability to act, to rescue herself or her loved ones. Without that power, her voice and desire remain irrelevant, and the novel lays itself open to the charge of being sensationalistic.

In *Surfacing* the heroine's lack of confidence, her sense of herself as less than whole, was linked to her powerlessness, her sense of herself as victim. Offred, in contrast, is very much a fully formed subject with a strong sense of voice and desire, who remains nonetheless fully victimized by events beyond her control. This, it seems to me, is a spectacle at once more frightening and more troubling. The narrator of *Surfacing* learned, or appeared to learn, that to relinquish power (language, voice, and desire) is to accept the role of passive victim. In *The Handmaid's Tale* Offred lives the role of victim with voice and desire intact and fully formed. But that voice and desire provide her with no more access to power than that experienced by the woman in *Surfacing*. Offred, then, comes to differ very little from her predecessors, Isabel, Hester, Clarissa, and Tess. All are strong women who have lost control over their own lives and are held against their will. Their only remaining power is the power to move others. However, in *Handmaid's Tale*, unlike the earlier novels, the emotion constructed for us to feel is not so much love or sympathy as pain and outrage, a dull despair, so familiar as to have become a cliché. If in *Surfacing* there was a sense, however tentative, that the narrator might have learned to appropriate power and use it for herself, in *The Handmaid's Tale* we find that Offred's use of power is no further developed and is actually even more restricted. Again, I will be looking at this novel in terms of the three categories: desire, voice, and female rescue/heroism.

Linda Kauffman writes that "Offred narrates from exile, a ceaseless reiteration of her desire and her despair" (222). I would like to examine the connection between those two terms. In *The Handmaid's Tale* we are given a limited and uncritical view of desire. Its origin is mysterious; little attention is paid to its creation. Instead, it seems to be just *there*, a quantifiable substance. Desire exists before despair and despair, if anything, only augments desire.

The book opens in what had once been a high-school gym, and what Offred notes, "faintly like an afterimage," is the "yearning" that took place there: "There was old sex in the room and loneliness, and expectation, of something without a shape or name. I remember that yearning, for something that was always about to happen .... We yearned for the future. How did we learn it, that talent for insatiability. It was in the air; and it was still in the air" (13). The yearning of adolescents years ago is unsettling. Desire is what propels us forward, makes us want to *know* what comes next, to *do* what comes next. But Offred and the other women in the gym have no futures. They *are* what came next, and realistically can look forward to nothing better. The future for which they had all yearned has turned into a nightmare with no sign of an ending. It is this sense of doom that the dystopia brings, the sense of the future as the end, that makes the novel so bleak. The desire of the adolescents "was in the air; and it was still in the air." The occupants still want, still maintain their "talent for insatiability," but in Gilead such emotion is outdated, vestigial.

For Offred, such desire is unsettling. If she could let it go, or even suppress and reroute it, she might be able to survive the society of Gilead, learn to live within its strictures. "Waste not want not. I am not being wasted. Why do I want?" she asks (17). She lives in a society where desire, because it expresses the will of the individual and because it is so unpredictable, can get a person into trouble. It gets her commander into trouble. Offred recognizes this potential almost as soon as she is called into his study after hours: "But there must be something he wants, from me. To want is to have a weakness. It's this weakness, whatever it is, that entices me. It's like a small crack in a wall, before now impenetrable. If I press my eye to it, this weakness of his, I may be able to see my way clear. I want to know what he wants" (128). "'I want ...' he says. I try not to lean forward. Yes? Yes yes? What, then? What does he want? But I won't give it away, this eagerness of mine. It's a bargaining session, things are about to be exchanged" (130). Offred continues "to want" even when there seems no hope of any gain, even though she can see no reason for it. Instead, she leans toward the commander hoping to find in his desire a clue or a way out. She wants to know what he wants.

Unproductive, potentially dangerous, where does this desire come from? The desire represented in *The Handmaid's Tale* seems to be both a natural occurrence (something teenagers used to feel in the old days, and something which people still cannot help but feel even if they do not understand it) *and* a direct response to the prohibitions and restrictions of her situation. Offred returns from a "salvaging," a group killing and extermination of one scapegoated figure, and reports: "But also I'm hungry. This is monstrous, but nevertheless it's true. Death makes me hungry. Maybe it's because I've been emptied; or maybe it's the body's way of seeing to it that I remain alive, continue to repeat its bedrock prayer: *I am, I am.* I am, still. I want to go to bed, make love, right now. I think of the word *relish*. I could eat a horse" (293). It is this appetite for existence, "bedrock prayer: *I am, I am*," which drives her to tell her story. Her voice is the manifestation of this desire. Her desire gives her voice; she gives voice to her desire.

One of the characteristics of desire is that no matter how unfocused it may be, it seeks an object. That object may be a particular lover, it may be recognition by others, or (as in the example above) it may be food. Desire needs a target or object. For Offred that target/object becomes her imagined listener or reader. She feels the hopelessnes of such a desire acutely because there may be no one there: "But if it's a story, even in my head, I must be telling it to someone. You don't tell a story only to yourself. There's always someone else.Even when there is no one ... I'll pretend you can hear me. But it's no good, because I know you can't" (49-50). Desire without hope, a voice without a listener. All avenues are blocked, all exits closed. We are given here a representation of female desire as a force, no matter how strong, that remains blocked and impotent.

What gives Offred hope is her reception of another message, sent out almost as blindly as her own. She finds some words, "*Nolite te bastardes carborundorum*," (Don't let the bastards grind you down) scratched in a corner of her closet (62). In order to find that message she has had to examine, piece by piece, every corner of her room. The message cheers her and gives her hope. It gives her reason to narrate her own words, for someone else to receive, someone as unknown as she was to this writer.

Telling her story is not easy: "Nevertheless it hurts me to tell it over, over again. Once was enough: wasn't once enough for me at the time? But I keep going on with this sad and hungry and sordid, this limping and mutilated story, because after all I want you to hear it, as I will yours too if I ever get the chance, if I meet you or if you escape, in the future or in Heaven or in prison or underground, some other place ... By telling you anything at all I'm at least believing in you, I believe you're there, I believe you into being. Because I'm telling you this story I will your existence. I tell, therefore you are" (279). She trusts the power of her voice to create the listener who will give her experience meaning. The future, if there is to be any, lies in the possibility of the listener's existence. Just as she fulfilled the role of unknown but not unimagined listener for the last handmaid, the one who had scrawled the phrase in the closet, so she hopes for a listener for her own story. The listener has to be outside Gilead, in "some other place." She posits a reader/listener outside her nightmare and thereby reassures herself that there *is* an outside, a place beyond her terrible now. Our very act of reading her words, therefore, becomes a kind of rescue.

It is the intensity of her desire for a place and a reader beyond which makes the epilogue's "Historical Notes" so ironic and so grim. What is probably most chilling about them is Professor Pieixoto's manner of taking Offred's pain so lightly. The readers' first sense upon realizing that we are somewhere outside of and beyond Gilead is the relief of waking from a nightmare (it did all end). She/we have been rescued. The relief, however, is short lived, turning to astonishment and dismay that so much seems to have been forgotten. The scholars at the Twelfth Symposium on Gileadean Studies in the year 2195 feel none of Offred's pain and despair. They are not the listeners she had imagined. By codifying and objectifying all of the information, her tale has been emptied of all human warmth, urgency and desperation.[21]

The effect of Offred's voice being swallowed up and countered by Pieixoto's should by now be familiar to us from our readings of the other novels. The "bad" response of the academics of the future assures our "good" and "correct" response. Our feelings for the heroine are enhanced by our sense that she has not only been mistreated; she has also been misread. It seems to me that Offred is constructed in this novel exactly as Tess, Clarissa, Isabel, and Hester were in theirs. Offred's interiority is constructed through the text's representation of her voice and her desire. Thoroughly strong and thoroughly victimized, she speaks and she wants, but is unable to act. Through her account, the reader comes to see as she sees and to feel as she feels; we begin, in short, to identify with her. That is why Professor Pieixoto's cold and detached report on her life shocks us. It is a brutal exteriorization, the effect of which is to heighten our pity for the heroine and our outrage on her behalf. This method of a constructed closeness and familiarity with our heroine, followed by a radical distancing and defamiliarization, is used in all the novels considered so far.[22]

In this Atwood novel, unlike the earlier *Surfacing*, the fact of victimization does not block the heroine from locating her desire. In fact, it seems to help her: "Death," she says, "makes me hungry." (Ralph had said to Isabel, "There's nothing makes us feel so much alive as to see others die.") In full possession of her voice, she feels compelled to tell her story again and again: "Wasn't once enough for me at the time? But I keep on going with this sad and hungry and sordid, this limping and mutilated story." The effort seems exhausting and pointless. The effect is something like a Beckett play in which voice and desire drone on and on, long after there is anything worth saying, anything worth getting, long after all hope is gone. Unable to act, whether to save herself or her daughter, she remains locked in her victimization. With Nick's help she escapes to Canada. But the effect of the epilogue is to annul any relief we might have gained at the thought of her escape.

In what way, we may ask, is the sense of hopelessness imbued by *Handmaid's Tale* any different from the sense created by *The Portrait of a Lady*? One difference is that we have no sense in this twentieth-century text that the heroine has "asked for" or sought out her punishment (except to the extent that she was politically uninvolved before – had felt alienated from her mother's feminist politics). But ultimately do we not still feel, as we did in *Portrait*, confined, fixed, and stifled? We are outraged certainly, but are we empowered? I don't think so. It seems more likely that this book has merely reinscribed and in some ways strengthened the emotions and the responses generated through the earlier novels: helpless outrage at the treatment of an innocent female. Readers have often found Richardson's novels to be virtually pornographic in their minute discussion of female victimization. Is this novel any less so? Isn't it another exploitation of female victimization for literary thrills and chills?

One possible clue to the arrested potential in Atwood's work might lie in her representation of the alienated relationship between mothers and daughters. At a climactic moment in *Surfacing* the narrator is granted a glimpse of the mother who had died several years earlier: "Then I see her. She is standing in front of the cabin ... she is turned half away from me, I can see only the side of her face ... She turns her head quietly and looks at me, past me, as though she knows something is there, but she can't quite see it" (182). Face half turned away, looking past her daughter without seeing her: this scene seems emblematic of all the missed connections and awkward distances between mother and daughter in this novel. The mother who scared away a bear, who rescued a drowning brother, and who disappears for hours in the bush is always remote. When the narrator sees her mother's diary on a hospital bedside table, she thinks, "All she put in it was a record of the weather and the work done on that day: no reflections, no emotions" (22), and filches it from her death bed: "I thought there might be something about me, but except for the dates the pages were blank" (22). This is a mother whose feelings for her daughter, whose feelings about *anything*, are mysterious. What did her mother want? the narrator, echoing Freud, might ask. That question is unanswerable – the mother is gone – but it is possible that the distance and coolness of the mother offers us a clue to the numbness of the daughter. Without access to her mother's desire, the daughter cannot reach or use her own.

The narrator in *Surfacing* cannot reach her mother. The narrator of *The Handmaid's Tale* can reach neither mother *nor* daughter. When Offred exclaims, "I want her back. I want everything back, the way it was. But there is no point to it, this wanting" (132), she is referring, most pointedly, to her mother, to wanting to try again to reach her. In that sense, Offred has no trouble knowing what she wants (she wants her mother and "everything back"), and has no trouble expressing that desire, but without the ability to act, desire and voice are impotent and pointless. She can get no one back.

The central horror in this book of horrors is the loss of Offred's daughter. In an earlier chapter I referred to two critics, J. Hillis Miller and John Goode, both of whom confessed that parts of *Tess* were so unbearably painful as to be impossible to read. The section in which Offred's daughter is taken from her causes me the same readerly pain. "Of all the dreams," Offred says, "this is the worst" (85). I would agree and would suggest that it is around this central loss that the entire novel is organized. Her longing for the child that is gone, her feelings of hopelessness at ever seeing her again, ever getting her back, are part of the overall misery of Gilead where many women long for children to love and for the children who will give them a future. But there is, at least for Offred, a longing for the mother as well when she wails, "I want her back. I want everything back, the way it was. But there is no point to it, this wanting." Her desire is palpable and painful, but so, alas, is her sense of futility.

Offred wants to reclaim the past, "everything back the way it was," but since this is a dystopia, a novel set in a hypothetical and bleak future, *her* desire for the past is actually a desire for *our* present. We are the time before; we have now that which she can never have again. What we have is a possibility for connection, freedom and security that is both within our grasp and (at least according to the vision of this novel) already lost to us.[23] Through our identification with the heroine we are inducted into her desire and into her pain, her sense of futility that "there's no point to it, this wanting."

The recurring images of mothers and daughters and their inability to connect with, or help, each other, may produce a clue to the locked and frozen stasis of Atwood's nightmarish fictional realm. Unable to reach or to know their mothers' desire, Atwood's heroines' own desire remains impotent and pointless. They are trapped in a world of paranoia and helplessness.[24] Mothers and daughters figure also in Angela Carter's work, work which seeks a way out of this deadlock.[25]

ANGELA CARTER

"The Bloody Chamber"

I will focus here on only one of the stories in this collection, the title piece, a stunning and troubling reworking of the Bluebeard story.[26] As Carter tells it, this is the story of a young woman's initiation into a "desire that is not her own," her seduction into complicity with that desire, and of her eventual rescue from its cruel effects. As an extended study of the construction of female desire around the desire of the other (a desire here that is violent and sadistic), the story flirts dangerously with the pornographic, for by identifying with the heroine we are being asked to identify with that sadistic desire as well.

The story opens with the heroine-narrator on a train heading for the castle of her new husband. Because it is her first night away from her mother, she feels torn between her quickening desire for her husband and her remembered affection for her mother: "In the midst of my bridal triumph, I felt a pang of loss as if ... I had, in some way, ceased to be her child in becoming his wife" (7–8). Before turning her full attention to the husband, the narrator dwells, for a moment, on her mother, remembering her as a hero: "My eagle-featured, indomitable mother; what other student at the Conservatoire could boast that her mother had outfaced a junkful of Chinese pirates, nursed a village through a visitation of the plague, shot a man-eating tiger with her own hand and all before she was as old as I?" (7). The mother had sacrificed everything to marry for love, but it is not at all clear that her daughter is following the same path. On the contrary, it seems that she may be marrying only to secure wealth for her impoverished family, that she may even see this as a type of heroism worthy of justifying her own sacrifice and immolation. However, even if it was wealth which had first drawn her to the marriage, it is her husband's desire for her which ultimately lures her. She is pulled by it, almost against her will: "And it was as though the imponderable weight of his desire was a force I might not withstand, not by virtue of its violence but because of its very gravity" (9). No sooner does she recognize his desire than she experiences the birth of her own, for hers is a desire which is solely, it would appear, based on his. Once awakened, her own desire is formed according to the patterns his provides. His is sadistic; hers becomes masochistic. He wishes to possess and kill her; she finds herself strangely mesmerized by this plan.

The fiancé gives her a wedding gift, "A choker of rubies, two inches wide, like an extraordinarily precious slit throat" (11). The necklace is important, not only as a prefiguration of her intended fate, but also as her initiation into his gaze and his desire: "I saw him watching me in the gilded mirrors with the assessing eye of a connoisseur inspecting horseflesh ... When I saw him look at me with lust, I dropped my eyes but in glancing away from him, I caught sight of myself in the mirror. And I saw myself, suddenly as he saw me ... I saw how that cruel necklace became me. And, for the first time in my innocent and confined life, I sensed in myself a potentiality for corruption that took my breath away" (11). To see herself "suddenly as he saw me" is to adopt the male gaze, to internalize his vision of her until it becomes her own.

The story thus becomes not simply the story of one woman's seduction, but an account of the creation of female masochistic desire:[27] "No. I was not afraid of him; but of myself. I seemed reborn in his unreflective eyes, reborn in unfamiliar shapes ... I blushed again, unnoticed, to think he might have chosen me because ... he sensed a rare talent for corruption" (20). Carter introduces an ambiguity here. Until this point, the account seemed to imply that female masochism develops in response to male sadism, but here a new sense is introduced, the idea that the narrator (and thus all women?) has a "talent" for this corruption, is somehow innately "good at it." Ideas such as these in Carter's early work have proved contentious.

The narrator is taken with what she sees of herself in the mirror, admires herself and sees how good she looks as a victim. The lesson in desire continues until it becomes increasingly difficult to say whether she has any desire or volition left of her own. It is only after their wedding night that she gets the fateful bunch of keys. The sequence of events is important because her curiosity is depicted as neither independent nor innocent, but as sexual, as part of her growing complicity in her husband's desire. When he leaves her alone with the keys, he (purposefully) leaves her in a state of newly-aroused sexuality. Her desire and her curiosity have only been stirred and woken up. They are not yet sated, not yet even understood: "I felt a vague desolation that within me ... there had awoken a certain queasy craving like the cravings of pregnant women for the taste of coal or chalk or tainted food, for the renewal of his caresses. Had he not hinted to me, in his flesh as in his speech and looks, of the thousand, thousand baroque intersections of flesh upon flesh? I lay in our wide bed accompanied by, a sleepless companion, my dark newborn curiosity" (22). Hers is a dark curiosity eager to know more about the dark side of love. She describes it as "baroque," and "queasy," a craving slightly decadent and slightly sick. It is, at least in part, a desire to learn more about her husband that leads her down the dark corridors in search of the forbidden room. She wants, she says, to find his "real life' (25), his "real self" (26), his "soul" (27). Female curiosity, particularly as it is enacted in this story, in apparent contravention of the husband's wishes, might appear heroic. After all, it signals independence, resourcefulness, even rebellion. But whose desire is the heroine enacting? Whose curiosity is she seeking to satisfy? By this point her own desire has become virtually indistinguishable from her husband's. She has started to want what he wants: "I knew I had behaved exactly according to his desires ... I had been tricked into my own betrayal ... The secret of Pandora's box; but he had given me the box, himself, knowing I must learn the secret. I had played a game in which every move was governed by a destiny as oppressive and omnipotent as himself" (34).

Here Carter is weighing both the guilt versus innocence of the Eve or Pandora figure as well as the degree of her independence. Female curiosity, the desire to take initiative and act heroically, has rarely been validated in our culture. In this case, the heroine exerts her curiosity to seek her own doom. But in knowledge lies power.

Coming face to face with the inevitable results of her flirtation with corruption is sobering. She stares at the consequences of her husband's desire (a desire which has come close to being her own). By portraying the heroine as to some degree involved in her own destruction, Carter forces us to examine the extent to which women have complied with the system which oppresses them. She makes it more difficult for us and them to claim only the role of innocent, and thereby powerless, victim.

There is, however, a further surprising twist, another role for us to play. Just as the husband lifts his sword over the neck of his bride, there is an interruption: "You never saw such a wild thing as my mother, her hat seized by the winds and blown out to sea so that her hair was her white mane, her black lisle legs exposed to the thigh, her skirts tucked round her waist, one hand on the reins of the rearing horse while the other clasped my father's service revolver, and behind her, the breakers of the savage indifferent sea, like the witnesses of a furious justice" (39-40). The mother charges in heroically, and somewhat comically. She comes in like a mock-heroic *deus ex machina*. She, who had killed a tiger at eighteen, wastes no time in killing her son-in-law with her husband's gun. The mother has appropriated the position of rescuing hero as easily as she stole the horse "from a bemused farmer" (40), as easily as she wields her dead husband's revolver.

The ending, an abrupt and stunning reversal, may complicate more than it solves. The story relies on two contradictiory impulses, twin desires. On the one hand the heroine is lured to near-death through her induction into a desire that is explicitly self-destructive. On the other hand she is saved from the final effect of this desire by a mother who swoops in from nowhere to pluck her from danger. Two desires, both female, exist side by side and in seeming contradiction; one is the desire to be seen, possessed, and destroyed, the other is the desire to preserve, to protect, and to rescue. How are we to understand the relationship between these seemingly contradictory forces? Does the mother's rescue provide us with a happy-ever-after conclusion, or has Carter's obsession with violent sexuality left us with a vision much darker? Have we been granted a vision of female possibility and heroism, or is it just the same old story told once again?

Critics have been quick to point out the contradictions inherent in this and the other stories in *The Bloody Chamber*. A number of them assert that the problem may lie in the form itself. In her attempt to rewrite or "talk back" to the fairy tales, Carter sometimes seems merely to repeat rather than re-invent sexual stereotypes.[28] It is as if the tales take on a life of their own and start to tell themselves with a narrative drive toward conformity that resists any attempt of the author to take control and tell them in a new way or steer them in a different direction.

There is, however, at the climactic moment in the story, a moment of liberation, a moment – however stylized and unrealistic – in which freedom is at least imagined. When the mother bursts onto the scene of her daughter's execution, the narrator compares this interruption to a hypothetical interruption of an opera wherein, just at the moment of greatest tragedy and pathos, the hero bursts into a "jaunty aria" and announces that "bygones were bygones, crying over spilt milk did nobody any good and, as for himself, he proposed to live happily ever after" (39). We can laugh at such a bizarre juxtaposition of comedy and tragedy, but I think Carter's intention is quite serious. What if, she is saying, we *could* let bygones be bygones, if we *could* free ourselves from history? Her critics might point out that this collection demonstrates the difficulty or even impossibility of such an escape, that it proves how deeply we are mired in history's self-destructive fantasies and thus doomed to repeat them. But Carter's fiction *does* force us to re-assess the motives and forces behind women's all too frequent assumption of the role of victim; it urges us to refuse that role and take responsibility for living differently.

Nights at the Circus

What if, like the operatic hero described in "The Bloody Chamber," we decide to let bygones be bygones and propose to live happily ever after? How can we imagine such release from the recurring narrative patterns of female victimization in which the very stories become eroticized or charged in such a way that they serve merely to create the pattern anew? I see Angela Carter's *Nights at the Circus* as an attempt to imagine just these possibilities.

Carter's writing has been called "magic realism,"[29] and, for want of a better term, it will do to describe the world of imaginative possibility, mystery and magic which she creates. *Nights at the Circus* is an attempt to imagine new possibilities, new ways to tell the story. The attempt is tentative; we are offered no system of redemption or liberation. Instead, Carter works gingerly, and with considerable humour, to tease out radical possibilites for transformation in the here and now.[30]

A novel of transformation differs from a utopian novel in that it describes, not the perfect state, not that which "comes after," but the liminal state, that which exists between one state and another. *Nights at the Circus*, like *Surfacing*, is obsessed with borders. But if the emphasis in Atwood's novel was on lines which divide and separate, here the emphasis is on moments of liminality, on places and states which have no lines, that are *both* this *and* that, both here *and* there.

This liminality is exemplified both in the novel's characters and in its setting. The heroine, Fevvers, is a woman (probably), but she has wings (almost certainly). Her foster mother and companion, Lizzie, is both a Marxist revolutionary (most likely) and a magician (probably). The uncertainties are as deliberate as they are unresolved. Carter plays throughout with the notion of secret identities and confidence tricks. Similarly, the novel is situated, both geographically and historically, in a liminal no man's land. Much of it takes place on the steppes of Russia (*between* Europe and Asia) when a circus train heading from London to Japan, via St Petersburg, is blown up in Siberia.

But it is in its sense of time that the novel is most "liminal," that is, most disorienting. When Walser, the hero, first meets Fevvers, he is shaken to realize that he hears Big Ben ring midnight at least twice in succession. The reader suffers from the same disorientation, the same sense that we are falling through cracks in time, that time may occasionally slip or double back on itself. With a time frame which stretches from October 1899 to 1 January 1900, the novel trembles on the cusp of the century, poised like the heroine of *Surfacing*, half in one state and half in the other. The drama of the moment is deliberately played up: "For we are at the fag-end, the smouldering cigar-butt, of a nineteenth century which is just about to be ground out in the ashtray of history. It is the final, waning, season of the year of Our Lord, eighteen hundred and ninety nine. And Fevvers has all the éclat of a new era about to take off" (*Nights* 11). Something old is just about finished, ground down, smoked up. There is a chance for something new and Fevvers is very obviously something new.

Set at the turn of one century and written at the turn of the next (the book was published in 1984), Carter's novel has an apocalyptic urgency, an impatience to toss out the old and get on with the new.[31] Everywhere the chance to start from scratch is emphasized. As Lizzie says to Fevvers, "You never existed before. There's nobody to say what you should do or how to do it. You are Year One. You haven't any history and there are no expectations of you except the ones you yourself create" (198). No history, no expectations, no rules: she, like the coming century, is a blank slate. The novel explores the possibilites and the terrors of blankness, of beginning again from nothing.

Like Fevvers, we are encouraged to start all over again, but are never told that it will be easy. On the contrary, it is strongly suggested that only fools accept such undertakings. The book is saved from utopian didacticism and simplemindedness by its humour and sense of bitter and complex ironies, not the least of which is the fact that the brave new world that Fevvers is to inherit is the century of violence, destruction, and horror through which we have just passed. Hope is itself undertaken as a challenge (and a nearly hopeless one at that). At one point Fevvers starts to wax eloquent in the style of all the orators, playwrights, and politicians of the past century who have promised us liberation and hope: "And once the new world has turned on its axle so that the new dawn can dawn, then, ah, then! all the women will have wings, the same as I. This young woman ... will tear off her mind-forged manacles, will rise up and fly away. The doll's house doors will open, the brothels will spill forth their prisoners, the cages, gilded or otherwise, all over the world, in every land, will let forth their inmates singing together the dawn chorus of the new, the transformed" (285). Lizzie shuts her up with, "It's going to be a bit more complicated than that ... The old witch sees storms ahead ... You improve your analysis, girl, and *then* we'll discuss it" (286). This is not the only time Lizzie, the pragmatist and Marxist-magician, has to pull someone down to earth, for the novel is cluttered with dreamers and visionaries, each seeking transformation and liberation. There is a group of escaped female convicts who have broken free of a panopticon in Siberia (run by a woman). There is the group of anarchists who blow up the circus train under the mistaken impression that Fevvers is engaged to the Duke of Wales. There are the whores who burn down the whore-house when their beloved madam dies, and in Siberia, the characters meet "a well-educated man – boy I should say ... [who] never mentioned 'yesterday.' All *he* could talk of was 'tomorrow,' a shining morrow of peace and love and justice" (239). Lizzie scolds this man/boy as she has Fevvers, gives him a lecture on political realities, saying, " 'tomorrow never comes,' ... we live, always, in the here and now, the present" (239). *Nights at the Circus* explores that present, a past in which the future is always being born.

Making the impossible believable is the theme of the book. In this sense it is meta-fictional, for it is *about* confidence tricks, and is *itself* an extended confidence trick. To play a confidence trick on someone is to engage their trust. It is also to turn them into a dupe, a clown, or a fool. Walser, the journalist, sees himself as particularly immune to this fate. He decides to interview Fevvers in order to add her to his "series of interviews tentatively entitled: 'Great Humbugs of the World' " (11). Confronted by her, he tries to "keep his wits about him" (9), suspects there's "something fishy about the Cockney Venus" (8), but relies on both his "professional necessity to see all and believe nothing" (10) as well as "his habit of suspending belief" (10). But in part 1 all his defences are breached. He is seduced into belief, seduced by champagne, by Fevvers' enormous blue eyes, Lizzie's magic with the clocks, and most of all by Fevvers' tale; her voice and story enchant him into a kind of tranced faith. Held by her spell, Walser here re-enacts the roles of Belford, Dimmesdale, Ralph, and Angel, all the male characters who were mesmerized by the plight of their heroines. However, this heroine is different. Although she undergoes terrible sufferings, there is a kind of comic surefootedness about her, a way of bouncing back from adversity that is more reminiscent of Moll Flanders than of Clarissa.

As in the other books, our identification is routed through the central male character, but here it is coded differently partly because Walser falls so hard for the heroine. He listens to Fevvers' fabulous tale, and despite himself "falls" for it. Looking into her eyes "he felt himself trembling as if he, too, stood on an unknown threshhold" (30). Falling in love and falling for a trick are virtually the same thing in this novel. They are, furthermore, virtually the same thing as *reading* any novel. "Shall I believe it," thinks, Walser.

"Shall I pretend to believe it?" (28). It doesn't matter whether he believes or just pretends to believe; the book is conducted on the threshold of love, seduction, and magic. We all have to fall if we want to read it.

In his pursuit of love Walser suffers indignities that Ralph Touchett or the Reverand Dimmesdale would never imagine. He becomes first a clown in the circus (he'll do anything to follow Fevvers) and then a fool. (Hit on the head in the train crash, he becomes mentally deranged.) At each successive stage he is more the stooge, the dupe, and the fool, until finally "he was a perfect blank" (222). At this point *he*, comically, enacts the role usually assigned to women. Found unconscious by the escaped female convicts, they wonder how to wake him: "'The old tales diagnose a kiss as the cure for sleeping beauties,' said Vera, with some irony" (222). Wiped clean as a slate, he is at the end, a new man, ready to believe in and to love the new woman, Fevvers.

The reader is invited to identify with Walser, and, like him, learn to dance with the clowns, become a fool and get "tricked." There's a loss of dignity in such a fall, a dignity which the characters in the other novels succeeded in maintaining. For after all, in order to be seduced, to read a novel, to fall in love, or even to fly, we have to suspend our *disbelief* before we can even think about restoring or inventing our belief. We have to be willing to teeter on the threshhold and take the plunge.

But Walser does not command all the agency and all the active subjectivity in this novel. Indeed, as we have seen, his consciousness is "wiped clean"; he becomes "a perfect blank." Maybe blank is perfect in this world, the only way to start male-female relations anew. His erasure allows for the expression of Fevvers' full subjectivity and desire. Near the end of the novel, she finds him stumbling over the steppes, lost and deranged. Her excitement causes her wings to burst out in a manner that is comically both masculine *and* feminine: "I spread. In the emotion of the moment, I spread. I spread hard enough, fast enough to bust the stitching of my bearskin jacket. I spread, and out shot my you-know-whats" (251). Carter deliberately uses and confuses terminology for male and female sexual response. The wings are phallic, vaginal, and breastlike. Because they are like all of the above and none of the above, Fevvers' desire is represented as liminal and nonrestricted. It is something new, something other, that remains nonetheless familiar.

If Fevvers has a problem, it is that as liminal creature, she can become more idea than reality.[32] Like other women before her, she might be more valuable as symbol than as an actual being. It is as symbol or freak that she has been sought after and displayed in Ma Nelson's whore-house and Madame Schreck's house of horrors. It is her very liminality that leads Mr Rosencreutz to want to capture, possess, and kill her. It is he who describes her as "Queen of ambiguities, goddess of in-between states, being on the borderline of species" (81). These are the qualities that make her valuable, a collector's item to both Rosencreutz and later the Grand Duke.

Lizzie treats her as real, scolding her, feeding her, fussing over her like a mother, but even Walser, Walser who loves her, and who in many ways stands in for the reader, even he is unsure of just what it is he is loving. "She owes it to herself to remain a woman, he thought. It is her human duty. As a symbolic woman, she has a meaning, as an anomaly, none" (161). The problem is that as a "marvellous monster" she is "an exemplary being denied the human privilege of flesh and blood, always the object of the observer, never the subject of sympathy, an alien creature forever estranged" (161). A circus performer, a six foot two woman with wings, she is a marvellous object to behold, but to move beyond objectification, she must be, at least sometimes, "the subject of sympathy." Without demeaning or belittling her, such sympathy can bring her into the human fold, help us to believe that she really is one of us.

Fevvers exists in a liminal state between reality and illusion. There is deliberate confusion about how much her reality resides in our conception of her and how much is essentially hers. We are made to wonder whether there is anything beyond what we imagine of her. It is possible that she exists purely as "woman as sign," as empty as all the other heroines we have encountered so far. When she wanders in the Siberian wilderness, she longs to "see, once again, the wonder in the eyes of the beloved and become whole" (285). She needs to feel the wonder in Walser's gaze (and perhaps our own) to feel real again and complete. As a performer and lover she only feels whole when seen and appreciated, but there is a danger in this need to be held in the eyes of the other. At the climactic moment in the novel Fevvers experiences such a danger when in the Shaman's hut, she "felt that shivering sensation which always visited her when mages, wizards, impresarios came to take away her singularity as though it were their own invention, as though they believed she depended on their imagination in order to be herself. She felt herself turning, willy-nilly, from a woman into an idea" (289). It is this terrifying prospect which leads her to ask "Am I fact? Or am I fiction? Am I what I know I am? Or am I what he thinks I am?" (290). To feel oneself turn from woman into idea is to exist solely in the mind of another and to lose all other subjectivity. To prove herself, to find herself, and to find her answer, she spreads her wings. She notes with satisfaction the thrill such a spectacle provides her audience: "She cocked her head to relish the shine of the lamps, like footlights, like stage-lights; it was as good as a stiff brandy, to see those footlights, and, beyond them, the eyes fixed upon her with astonishment, with awe, the eyes that told her who she was" (290).

Fevvers is a performer who feels most real when she is held in the gaze of the worshipping audience. This is all the sympathy she needs. As neither monster nor angel nor human, she is none of the above and *all* of the above. She exists most fully held in our appreciative gaze, but if we try to dominate her, turn her from a woman into an idea, or hold her in any category (the "gilded cage" in this novel), she will resist. Like Walser, we readers will have to "start all over again" the process of knowing and loving her. As Walser puts it, "everything seemed to happen to me in the third peson as though, most of my life, I watched it but did not live it. And now, hatched out of the shell of unknowing by a combination of a blow on the head and a sharp spasm of erotic ecstasy, I shall have to start all over again" (294). Carter's novel seeks to deliver that same sort of blow and that same sort of spasm to us, its readers. It takes such eruptions to disassemble and reconstruct the old pathways of our desires and identification. She asks us all to start anew.

The novel ends with Fevvers' joyous laughter. She says to Walser, "'To think I really fooled you!' she marvelled. 'It just goes to show there's nothing like confidence'" (295). The confidence that women seek has perhaps first to be thought of as "just a trick." Is it fact or is it fiction? The question reverberates throughout the novel. The answer is that through our fictions we make our facts. Imagining that we might fly may give us all the confidence we need.

7 Postscript

The connection between women and the novel is a pervasive one. As its heroines, its authors, and its readers, we women have in many ways made the novel a genre of our own. And yet, as Nancy Miller notes at the end of her study of the heroine in the eighteenth-century novel: "Despite their titles and their feminine 'I,' it is not altogether clear to me that these novels are about or for women at all."[1] The novels, she suggests, are written by men for men, are "a masculine representation of female desire produced ultimately for an audience not of women readers, but of men" (150).

While Miller may be right, and I feel that in a number of ways she is, women have not, by and large, *felt* excluded from the novel. Miller may claim that "the feminocentric text made one of the great traditions of the novel possible; women are its predominant signifiers, but they are also its pretext" (150), but whether as text or pretext, as reality or illusion, women *have* seen themselves in novels. They have lived through novels, have used novels to understand their lives.[2]

It seems to me that we can get closer to the heart of this conundrum by addressing – once again – the relationship between identification and difference. We (both women and men) go to novels to discover ourselves, and that discovery, paradoxically, is effected largely through an experience of otherness. The novels studied here provide that experience; they are a place in which we see and feel for the other.

All novels are structured around some kind of difference. This was Bakhtin's point when he differentiated the novel from the epic. The novel, he pointed out, disrupts the monologism of the epic by including the parodic or mocking voice. The dialogism, which is essential to the novel, is, in one sense, already written into the split between the first and third persons. The novelist writes, "he did," "she felt" and we experience the words (and we suspect in many cases that he or she experiences them as well) as "*I* did," "*I* felt." I mentioned in the introduction Poulet's citation of Rimbaud's "Je est un autre."[3] This statement captures the ambiguity I seek to describe, the sense that in a novel we are perched, stranded even, in a no man's land between the first and the third persons. We learn through a *he* or *she* what *I* feels like.

That sense of difference and identification is accentuated through the difference of gender. Two of what are considered to be the first novels in English, Samuel Richardson's *Clarissa* and Daniel Defoe's *Moll Flanders* were created out of such a difference and a doubleness: in each case a male author speaks in and through a female voice, expressing her desire, feeling her emotion. In *Narrative Transvestism: Rhetoric and Gender in the Eighteenth-Century Novel*, Madeleine Kahn formulates what she sees as the central question "about a male author's use of a female narrative voice – What did he have to gain from the attempt? What is the point of creating a rather elaborate narrative structure to gain access to a voice on the other side of the structural divide between genders?" (10). My point is that that "structural divide" is essential for the construction not just of gender, but of desire and, therefore, of the novel itself.

Novels are places where difference is both constructed and preserved. Without difference there could be neither identification nor desire. Difference fuels our desire to see and to know, and to the extent that it animates and empowers us, it makes men of us (male and female readers alike).

I use two metaphors to describe the process of cross-gender identification as I understand it, site and role. Readers take up *sites* within the text,[4] and readers play *roles* within each text. These sites and roles, while explicitly gendered, are, nevertheless, temporary and interchageable; no one has to remain in one place for very long. Through identification, we take on roles presented to us in the text.

The reader's role is performative. The female reader, as we have seen, must often perform as male. This female identification with the male gaze has been well documented (Culler, Fetterley, Showalter for literature; de Lauretis, Doane, Mulvey for film). The novels studied here depend upon such identification, but they are also – and perhaps even more firmly – grounded in male identification with the female.

Identification with the female grants the reader access to realms of display and emotion often denied to the male. While the male site is the more openly privileged, the female site grants us a power of its own. Not only do readers gain a sense of interiority through experiencing the pain of the female other; we are also granted the power of seduction. By identifying with victims, with objects of pathos, we get a sense of what it feels like to be the objects of *attention* as well. From this position the reader is able to experience, vicariously, the ability to seduce, to lure the gaze of the other. In attracting sympathy and pity, we attract attention, an attention that comes to feel like love.

The novels considered here span three centuries and several modes; they are epistolary, realist, science fiction.[5] What they have in common is their preoccupation with the heroine. The feminist reader, I have tried to argue, cannot read these texts without allowing her- or himself to be seduced, to take roles defined as masculine as well as feminine. But beyond seduction, how do female readers in particular read these and other novels and maintain at once our sense of otherness along with a sense of agency and subjectivity? We must, I would like to propose, take on the role of Bluebeard's last wife. In Angela Carter's rendition of the tale, the wife is marked indelibly with the imprint of the bloody key: "I knelt before him and he pressed the key lightly to my forehead ... and when I glanced at myself in the mirror, I saw the heart-shaped stain had transferred itself to my forehead, to the space between the eyebrows, like the caste mark of a brahmin woman. Or the mark of Cain" (36). Like that wife (and like Hester Prynne), we wear the mark of our difference and our identification with male desire. Thus marked and thus empowered, we continue, our curiosity unabated.

Notes

CHAPTER ONE

1 Samuel Richardson, *Clarissa*, 4 vols., Everyman Edition (London: J.M. Dent and Sons, 1932), 4:367. All subsequent references in the text will refer to this edition.

2 At this point my argument is closeley aligned with Wolfgang Iser's in *The Implied Reader*. Like him, I see the novel as manipulating the reader. Unlike Iser, I do not see this function as ultimately or singly under the author's control. Furthermore my own intent, unlike Iser's, is to draw attention to the social construction of emotional responses like sympathy. The novel in such a view becomes as much cultural producer as cultural production.

3 The emotion to which Belford refers in this particular instance is anger. (Lovelace is incensed by what he perceives as Belford's meddling in his affairs.) It is, nevertheless, reasonable to interpret Belford's reference as more inclusive, pointing beyond this particular instance and this particular emotional reaction. His design, we may infer, is the arousal of emotions beyond anger – sympathy, remorse, love, and despair – to name a few.

4 Sedgwick, *Between Men: English Literature and Male Homosocial Desire* 25–6. See also Luce Irigaray: "For woman is traditionally a use-value for man, an exchange value among men; in other words, a commodity ... Woman is never anything but the locus of a more or

less competitive exchange between two men," *This Sex which is not One*, 31–2.

5 Nicholas Hudson has coined the term "meta-response" to "refe[r] to the tendency of readers to duplicate responses already expressed by characters. He uses this term in "Arts of Seduction and the Rhetoric of *Clarissa*," 30.

6 Frank R. Giordano Jr., *"I'd Have My Life Unbe": Thomas Hardy's Self-Destructive Characters* 163. See also Evelyn Hardy's "The Self-Destructive Element in Tess's Character," 447–50.

7 V.S. Pritchett, *The Living Novel*, 28. For a fascinating analysis of this and other readings of *Clarissa* and *Tess*, see Ellen Rooney's "Criticism and The Subject of Sexual Violence."

8 I do not mean to imply that the critics are alone in blaming the heroines, in seeing them as to some degree "asking for it." There is ample evidence in each text for such a conclusion. I only want to point out the extent to which these critics have uncritically followed, and in some cases, extended the leads provided by the texts.

9 Foucault sees the "individual" in Western society as an "effect of power" and has written that "we should try to discover how it is that subjects are gradually, progressively, really and materially constituted through a multiplicity of organisms, forces, energies, material, desires, thought, etc.," *Power/Knowledge*, 97–8. Judith Butler explains that feminists have turned to the work of Lacan "in part ... to reassert the kind of symbolic constraints under which becoming 'sexed' occurs," *Bodies*, 95.

10 On the connection between Simone de Beauvoir and later French feminists, see Toril Moi's *Sexual/Textual Politics*, 98. For an analysis of the relation between the work of Beauvoir and Irigaray, see Judith Butler, *Gender Trouble*, 9–13.

11 For one among the many criticisms of this point of view, see Shoshana Felman, "Women and Madness," 3.

12 Irigaray herself stresses the inherent duality or plurality of woman in her punning title, *This Sex which is not One*.

13 Schor writes, "I share with many other middle-aged feminists a nostalgia for the first decade of feminist critique ... because it allowed feminist critics to reinvent the universal." "French Feminsim" 26.

14 Some of these titles consciously mime and echo one another: Diana Fuss's "Reading Like a Feminist" in *Essentially Speaking*, 23–37, for example, is a commentary on Peggy Kamuf's "Writing Like a Woman" (1980), Jonathan Culler's "Reading as a Woman" (1982),

and Robert Scholes's "Reading Like a Man" (1987). For a full
account of these works, see Fuss. After discussing these and other
works, Fuss concludes, "I read this piece *like* a feminist; what it
means to read as or even like a woman I still don't know" (26). The
following is a partial list of other titles on the subject: Shoshana Felman, *What Does a Woman Want: Reading and Sexual Difference*;
Elizabeth A. Flynn and Patrocinio P. Schweikart, *Gender and Reading: Essays on Readers, Texts, and Contexts*; Mary Jacobus, ed.,
Reading Woman: Essays in Feminist Criticism; Sara Mills, ed., *Gendering the Reader*; Pam Morris, "Re-Vision: Reading as a Woman"
and "Writing as a Woman" in *Literature and Feminism: An Introduction*. A personal note: one of those similar titles was my own. When I
wrote my Ph.D. dissertation in 1992, I titled it "Reading as a
Woman" and thought that I was original. At least I was in good com-
pany.

15 See part 1 of *Madwoman in the Attic*, by Gilbert and Gubar, 3-104.
Also, Tillie Olsen, *Silences*, and Elaine Showalter, *A Literature of
Their Own*.

16 This is where Foucault's analysis of power is so helpful. He abandons
the traditional polarization whereby a repressive monadic totality
overwhelms a powerless and therefore innocent entity, in favour of a
model in which power circulates so that it is exercised by all parties
and is as productive as it is destructive: "Power is employed and
exercised through a net-like organisation. And not only do individuals circulate between its threads; they are always in the position of
simultaneously undergoing and exercising this power. They are not
only its inert and consenting target; they are always also the elements
of its articulation. In other words, individuals are the vehicles of
power, not its points of application," *Power/Knowledge,* 98.

17 Originally published in *Screen*, it was later reprinted in several collec-
tions, including Mulvey's *Visual and Other Pleasures*. All page references are to Mulvey's text.

18 See, for example, Patricia White's "Female Spectator, Lesbian
Specter," in Fuss's *Inside/Out*. Other works which deal with oppositional subject positions include Douglas's *Where the Girls Are*, Prib-
am's *Female Spectators*, and Walter's *Material Girls*.

19 Foucault, 1972, 115, quoted in *Essentially Speaking*, 32.

20 Lacan, *Ecrits*. See, especially, "The Mirror Stage," 1-7.

21 Gardiner, *Rhys, Stead, Lessing, and the Politics of Empathy*, 2. Her
reference to Chodorow is taken from *The Reproduction of Mother-*

ing: Psychology and Sociology of Gender (Berkeley: University of California Press, 1978), 167.

22 This is also noted by Lacan in *Ecrits*, 23. Fuss notes the same reference (*Identification Papers*, 143).

CHAPTER TWO

1 In the introduction, I spoke of the novel as a type of social agent whose work it is to create the "subject-effect," that sense of ourselves as potent and active agents, able to feel and to move. The role through which we experience that subjectivity in novels is almost always masculine.

2 The *O.E.D.* (Shorter, Third Edition) gives several definitions of the verb "to try." These include:
"#2. To separate the good part of a thing from the rest, esp. by sifting or straining, hence to sift or strain. Usu with *out* – 1790."
"#3. To separate (metal) from the ore or dross, by melting; to refine, purify by fire. Usu with *out* – 1686."
"#5. To ascertain, find *out* (something doubtful, obscure, or secret) by search or examination – 1761."
"#6. To determine the guilt or otherwise of (an accused person) by consideration of the evidence; to judge."
"#10. To subject to a severe test or strain; to put to straits, afflict – 1539."
All these uses are operative in *Clarissa*.

3 Diderot, "Eloge de Richardson," 130. The original French reads: "Depuis qu'ils me sont connus, ils ont été ma pierre de touche; ceux à qui ils déplaisent sont jugés pour moi," *Oeuvres de Diderot*, 1099. Of a woman who laughs at Clarissa rather than pitying her, he declares, "I say to you that this woman can never be my friend" (Lynch, 131). ("Je vous dis que cette femme ne peut jamais être mon amie" [Billy, 1100]).

4 Castle's insistence, for example, that Clarissa has been somehow silenced by the text – not allowed to speak – would seem to imply that there is a real, full-of-speech Clarissa awaiting rescue somewhere beyond the text's representaion of her. Warner seems to be imagining a similar, live, Lovelace when he writes: "Perhaps now he's mocking all our sentiment and seriousness" (54).

5 Diderot – "Oh Richardson! we become involved in your works, willingly or not; we become involved in the conversations" (Lynch, 121).

("O Richardson! on prend, malgré qu'on en ait, un rôle dans tes ouvrages, on se mêle à la conversation" [Billy, 1090]). See also John Preston, *The Created Self*, 38–93. Warner claims that "an unwary critic ... may discover himself playing a supporting role in an interpretive alliance directed by the text he intended to master" (3).

6 In *Samuel Richardson's Fictions of Gender*, Tassie Gwilliam's thesis is that "*Clarissa* becomes an analysis of masculinity through its analysis of femininity" (56), that the novel subverts "the commonly held belief that masculinity can operate independently of femininity ... or that it can be untainted by femininity" (56).

7 For more on Rousseau, women, and theatricality, see Rousseau's "Letter to M. d'Alembert" (83) and Fried (168-9). For an account of the historical background of the connection between femininity and theatricality see Laura Levine's "Men in Women's Clothing: Anti-theatricality and Effeminization from 1579 to 1642," 121–43.

8 For more on femininity and duplicity, see Gwilliam, 15-49.

9 Diderot, *Discours de la poésie dramatique*, 230, quoted and translated by Fried, 94, 217n.

10 Brecht is, of course, the exception that proves the rule for drama. Similarly the emphasis on artificiality and self-referentiality in some modern and post-modern works defy the tradition of naturalism or realism that was established in the eighteenth century. Nevertheless, almost all television and mainstream film narrative still rely on those conventions.

11 Marshall, *The Figure of Theater*, 190. This book provides an excellent and detailed look at Smith's philosophy.

12 According to James Carson, one of Samuel Richardson's goals as novelist was the promotion of sympathy for the moral and social good: "Imaginative identification is the central term in Richardson's ethics: Briefly, 'a feeling heart' produces sympathetic identification, which in turn promotes moral action" (99).

13 I agree with Gwilliam when she writes that "*Clarissa* becomes an analysis of masculinity through its analysis of femininity" (56). My own point is that masculinity in this novel is, in large part, constructed in response to the spectacle of female victimization.

14 These "attention markers," which tell us that others are paying attention and thus that we should too, appear throughout the text, but most noticeably in: "Every eye, in short, is upon you" (1:3), "All your acquaintance ... talk of nobody but you" (2:4), and "Every eye (as usual wherever you are ...) was upon you" (3:4).

15 At the time I write this, two trials are taking place. Both the O.J. Simpson trial in Los Angeles and the Paul Bernardo trial in Toronto remind me of the contemporary relevance of much of *Clarissa*. Each has been labelled a "circus," reminding us of our continued ambivalence about spectacle and entertainment, and each has been marked by controversy about how much of the evidence should be showed or played for the jury and media, reminding us of Clarissa's reluctance to be put on display. Finally, of course, both involve female victims and in each case the accused is often referred to as "charming" or "charismatic." The enormous interest generated by these trials reveals that the issues they raise – about sex, power, and violence – are deep and troublesome in our culture.

16 Warner writes that when Clarissa examines herself, "this is done by acting out a trial, in which Clarissa is at once defendant, prosecutor, and judge" (23–4).

17 In volume 1 Solmes is her target: "If my eyes would carry with them the execution which the eyes of the Basilisk are said to do, I would make it my first business to see this creature" (284). In volume 4 she is after Lovelace: "Oh, that I had the eye the basilisk is reported to have, thought I, and that his life were within the power of it! – directly would I kill him" (18-19). A basilisk is a mythological creature which was said to be able to kill with a look, an apt beast for this novel.

18 Of this trial scene, Gwilliam writes, "The trial seems to represent a chance to focus all eyes on his own spectacular presence, but it also signals the extent to which Lovelace's fantasies of power are inextricable from the power he locates in women" (78-9).

19 Foucault writes that "executions did not in fact frighten the people" but that, on the contrary, "the people never felt closer to those who paid the penalty than in those rituals intended to show the horror of the crime and the invincibility of power." Quite often, "the condemned man found himself a hero" (*Discipline and Punish*, 63, 67). Lennard Davis comments on the same popularization of the criminal in *Factual Fictions*: "The ritual of execution provides the criminal a platform from which to make his words public; the gibbet authorizes a form of publication by which the criminal's words are amplified" (126).

20 At the risk of repeating this too often, I want to point out the Rousseau-esque nature of Clarissa's speech. She incarnates his ideal of transparency. Foucault writes, "What in fact was the Rousseauist

dream that motivated many of the revolutionaries? It was the dream of a transparent society, visible and legible in each of its parts, a dream of there no longer existing any zones of darkness," *Power/Knowledge*, 152. For more on the connection between Rousseau and Foucault, see Martin Jay, *Downcast Eyes*, especially chapter 7, 381–434.

21 At this point Clarissa's reluctance or even inability to construct herself for another's view works in her favour. At other times it does not. See, for example, Lovleace's evaluation of her dislike of display: "A dear silly soul, thought I at the time, to depend upon the goodness of her own heart, when the heart cannot be seen into but by its actions" (3:64).

22 Clarissa does claim, however, that it was her own pride – wanting to be an example to others – that caused her downfall (2:378).

23 This is a running motif throughout the novel in which Lovelace sees himself as the hunter and Clarissa as the prey. There are numerous references to choose from. One among the many is found in volume 2 in which Lovelace compares his elaborate plots to the time and effort needed to snare "a simple linnet" (426).

24 It could be argued that we get a glimpse of real affection for Lovelace in the scene where he gives himself ipecacuanha to induce sickness (2:434–9), but the glimpse is so fleeting and so overlaid by all other incidents that it, like other of Lovelace's visions, becomes evanescent.

CHAPTER THREE

1 I am referring here to the concept of the "gaze" as a controlling and regulating force. See *Discipline and Punish* and *The Birth of the Clinic*. On the intellectual context out of which Foucault was working, see Martin Jay's *Downcast Eyes*. In chapter 2 I noted the way that thinkers such as Rousseau and Diderot worried about "theatricality," or what we might now call the "politics of the gaze."

2 There is a very real sense in which Hester disappears behind her mark. Pearl mockingly points this out when she shows her mother her distorted reflection in the armour at the governor's mansion. Nathaniel Hawthorne, *The Scarlet Letter* (New York: Norton, 1988), 73. All subsequent references in the text will refer to this edition.

3 The phrase is Foucault's; *Discipline and Punish*, 49.

4 David Marshall suggests "that our sympathy – and the pleasure we seem to take in it – depend on the violence and suffering inflicted on

those who appear as spectacles before us," *The Surprising Effects of Sympathy*, 48.

5 See, for example, Hunt, "*The Scarlet Letter*: Hawthorne's Theory of Moral Sentiments"; Hutner, *Secrets and Sympathy*; Male, "Hawthorne and the Concept of Sympathy"; and Michael, "History and Romance, Sympathy and Uncertainty."

6 A recent formulation of this traditional view is made by Janis B. Stout in "The Fallen Woman and the Conflicted Author: Hawthorne and Hardy." She writes, "When the character of the fallen woman is seriously and imaginatively treated, sympathy with her plight becomes a means of questioning not only the correctness of society's moral judgments of her, but the judgmental mentality itself" (234). For Stout, sympathy solves the problem, undoes the damage which society has inflicted.

7 See Dryden, *Nathaniel Hawthorne: The Poetics of Enchantment*: "Quite clearly, what [Hawthorne] seeks in the prefaces is both to attract and confuse his reader ... His veil at once conceals and entices the reader to imagine the features behind it" (125). Hutner also notes that "the dominant strategy of the preface is obfuscation rather than confession"(22), and comments on the "studied evasiveness of his style" (5–6).

8 In a footnote on page 88, Hunt writes, "We know that [Hawthorne] borrowed a copy of *The Theory of Moral Sentiments* from the Salem Athenaeum when he was in his early twenties." Male makes a similar assertion in footnote 4 on page 139.

9 The stigma remains today. "Don't make a spectacle of yourself," we warn children, particularly little girls. On being given such a warning, Mary Russo writes, "Making a spectacle of oneself seemed a specifically feminine danger." "Female Grotesques," 219.

10 See chapter 2 above for Rousseau and Diderot's views on women as spectacle.

11 This letter is quoted in Hutner, *Secrets and Sympathy* (7). The idea of having a heart that anyone may see through is reminiscent of Rousseau's desire for transparency with concomitant echoes of Bentham and panopticism; see chapter 2 above.

12 Leon Chai writes that "the American Renaissance is in one sense the final phase of Romanticism," *Romantic Foundations*, 6.

13 For the way Hawthorne uses this double gaze to connect Hester to witchcraft, see "Seduced by Witches: Nathaniel Hawthorne's *The Scarlet Letter* in the Context of New England Witchcraft Fictions."

14 This might account for the numerous snippets of "gossip" in the book. The narrator includes voices that are not his own, and from which he appears to want to distance himself, so as to allow the supernatural or the scandalous to be expressed: "It was whispered by those who peered after her that the scarlet letter threw a lurid gleam along the passage-way of the interior" (50). Also see the allegations against Chillingworth (88).

15 Goethe's *Elective Affinities* is a good example of the eighteenth century's fascination with both the social and the chemical properties of sympathy, as expressed in marriage and sexual attraction.

16 This is not to say that the aesthetic sense was alien to the eighteenth century. See Marshall, *The Surprising Effects of Sympathy* (3).

17 It may not be too far-fetched to suggest that the Romantic position of reader as poet or artist with active imaginative and sympathetic capabilities would be traditionally a male position. Paradoxically, if we are to take this image further, Hawthorne, by inviting that reader to "come into my depths" would appear to be taking a passive and stereotypically female position.

18 See Male, 139.

19 The sense that this "science" is not just old-fashioned but evil is underscored by the speculation on page 88 about Chillingworth's involvement with one Doctor Forman, alchemist and astrologer, in the murder of Sir Thomas Overbury.

20 See chapter 4.

21 Although Dimmesdale may feel as if Chillingworth is exposing him to the light, Hawthorne describes Chillingworth as working in the dark, as a miner or a gravedigger or a thief: "He groped along as stealthily, with as cautious a tread, and as wary an outlook, as a thief" (89).

22 Male writes that Chillingworth "anticipates the technique of modern psychiatry" (147).

23 Clarissa'a innocent transparency empowered her. Anyone, she said, was free to look into her heart. See chapter 2 above. Dimmesdale and Hawthorne are less at ease. They seek to arrange their revelations carefully.

24 In *Clarissa* such characters included the staring women who observe Clarissa's judicial appearance at Hampstead, and the "vulgar street swarmers" at Lovelace's imagined trial. See chapter 2 above. In *The Scarlet Letter*, it is the strangers who crowd around Hester in chapter 22 that we seek to differentiate ourselves from.

25 In this respect, Hawthorne reveals once more his Romantic heritage.

Abrams reminds us that for the Romantics, music replaced painting as the art with which literature was most often compared. Music was valued for its seemingly non-mimetic qualities (*The Mirror and the Lamp* 91–4).

26 In *The Blithedale Romance* the snooping narrator, Coverdale, overhears Zenobia: "And then I heard her utter a helpless sort of moan; a sound which, struggling out of the heart of a person of her pride and strength, affected me more than if she had made the wood dolorously vocal with a thousand shrieks and wails" (104). As in *The Scarlet Letter*, the medium by which emotion is communicated and recognized is sound not sight.

27 Male reminds us that "The significance which *sympathy* took on during this period seems to have stemmed from two important and interdependent developments; the striking discoveries in electricity and magnetism" (139).

28 As Foucault puts it, "Everyone must see punishment not only as natural, but in his own interest" (*Discipline and Punish*, 109).

29 See Carton, "'A Daughter of the Puritans'"; Herbert, "Nathaniel Hawthorne, Una Hawthorne, and *The Scarlet Letter*"; and Leverenz, "Mrs Hawthorne's Headache".

30 Quoted in Carton, 210.

31 Hawthorne may not have been unique in his reaction. See, for example, Catherine Gallagher who argues against accounts such as Gilbert and Gubar's which see authorship as an exclusivley male-defined activity. She argues that, on the contrary, writing was considered "degradingly female" and that since the Greek classical period there has been an "association of writing with femaleness in general and prostitution in particular." ("George Eliot and *Daniel Deronda*: The Prostitute and the Jewish Question," 40).

CHAPTER FOUR

1 Henry James, *The Art of the Novel*, 37.

2 Leo Bersani calls the prefaces "a model of structuralist criticism" ("The Jamesian Lie," 53). Also see Percy Lubbock, *The Craft of Fiction*. For a useful account of this tradition, and a deconstructive approach to it, see David Carroll, *The Subject in Question*.

3 For a study of power in James, see Mark Seltzer, *Henry James and the Art of Power*.

4 All references are to the Norton Critical Edition of *The Portrait of a*

Lady (New York: Norton 1975) which is based on the revised or "New York" edition of the novel, originally published in 1907.

5 Leo Bersani comments in "The Jamesian Lie" that "what we know [in James] we know through appreciation and not perception" (63–4).

6 Alfred Habegger sees *The Portrait* as "the product of a divided mind. James loves Isabel, loves her when she struggles to do the right thing under oppressive circumstance, loves her all the more because she is hamstrung by that fatal female mind" (*Henry James and the "Woman Business,"* 8).

7 See chapter 3 above.

8 Poirier also refers to "the chivalrousness and intelligence in [James's] treatment of Isabel ... Both James and Ralph can express an amused and mature tolerance of the heroine's vagaries" (195). (I might add the words "cautious" and "patronizing" to his more generous assessment.)

9 In a letter to his friend, Grace Norton, who noticed a similarity between Isabel and Minnie, James wrote: "You are both right & wrong about Minnie Temple. I had her in mind & there is in the heroine a considerable infusion of my impression of her remarkable nature. But the thing is not a portrait. Poor Minnie was essentially *incomplete* & I have attempted to make my young woman more rounded, more finished" (*Letters*, vol. 2 324). Also see Leon Edel's introduction to the Riverside Edition of *Portrait*, xv, and Habegger, 126–49.

10 Interestingly, Leon Edel in his introduction to the Riverside Edition of *Portrait of a Lady* notes that Minnie Temple "died at twenty-four of tuberculosis – like Ralph Touchett. James had loved her with the kind of love Ralph displays in the novel" (xv). This would seem to be evidence of a complex (and very Jamesian) type of cross-gender identification, with *both* Ralph *and* Minnie.

11 Henry James, "Letter to William James, 29 March 1870," *Letters*, vol. 1, ed. Leon Edel, 226.

12 *Letters*, vol. 1, 223.

13 Edel uses the very same phrase in his discussion of Isabel: "Isabel is a prisoner of her own constitutued self. She has been the victim of her own intelligence" (Riverside Introduction xx). He also writes, "She has been betrayed by her own inner nature" (xi).

14 "On the dramatic fitness – as one may call it – of her early death it seems almost idle to dwell. No one who ever knew her can have

failed to look at her future as a sadly insoluble problem – & we almost all had imagination enough to say ... that life – poor narrow life – contained no place for her" (*Letters*, vol. 1, 222).

15 Leon Edel comments on the similarities between James and Osmond in his introduction to the Riverside edition of the novel. He states: "Strange though it may seem, Gilbert Osmond expresses one side of his creator's character – the hidden side of Henry James: that side which loved power and sought to win it by his pen" (xii).

16 The theme of connoisseurship and dealership permeates the novel and is not entirely contained in the figures of Osmond and Ralph. Pansy's suitor, Rosier, is a collector, who, in an attempt to acquire her, sells almost all his other valuables. Other critics have noted this theme in the novel, but, like Annette Niemtzow (in "Marriage and the New Woman in *The Portrait of a Lady*"), they tend to see it as something which James was portraying only in order to condemn. See also Michael Gilmore's "The Commodity World of *The Portrait of a Lady*." Gilmore explores James's preparation of a "big" book which would bring him profits and prestige, and the way that that book itself deals with the commodification of individuals.

17 A number of recent studies have examined James' mercenary interests. These studies seek to redress the view which has presented James as a martyr to his art, as having a mind too lofty for petty interests such as money. They attempt to show that James was, on the contrary, very interested in both the financial and the social rewards of his position. *Portrait* was to be his first big book, his first chance to make his mark and make some money. We can see James, looking back in his preface, assessing and weighing the elements of that success.

On James' relationship to the profession of authorship see Michael Anesko, *"Friction with the Market": Henry James and the Profession of Authorship*; Michael Gilmore, "The Commodity World of *The Portrait of a Lady*"; and John Vernon, *Money and Fiction*.

18 It seems to me that an analogy could be developed here between James' aesthetic project and that of many modernists (visual and literary). Much of what we are instructed to value in modernism (I am thinking here particularly of photography and poetry) is the caught moment, the poetry in the mundane, the significance in the insignificant. Such work presents this "problem" as part of its very mastery. If we think of W.C. Williams' "This is just to say I have eaten the plums" or Picasso's bull's head made out of a bicycle seat and handle-

bars, we have examples of art which relish the disjunction in status between the ordinary object and the work of art. Even as they try to shock, works of art such as these seem to be also pointing in two other directions: to the "eye" of the artist who can see the beauty others miss, and to the beauty and power inherent in the everyday objects themselves.

19 The references to "plots" and "snares" echo the vocabulary in *Clarissa*.

20 "She wishes to be free and your bequest will make her free," he says to his father (160).

21 William Veeder offers a different view. His contention that "James leaves Isabel suspended between departure and arrival, poised between separation and commitment" ("The Feminine Orphan and the Emergent Master," 197) seems to me both compelling and accurate. By having her disappear as she does, James is able to have it both ways. In Veeder's words, Isabel is left suspended between commitment and isolation. I should say that she's left in a place of existential loneliness, that she finds a kind of freedom within the house of dumbness and suffocation.

22 See James's comment about his cousin: "Poor Minnie was essentially *incomplete* & I have attempted to make my young woman more rounded, more finished" (Letter to Grace Norton, Habegger, 160.)

23 Isabel refers to her benefactor as "the beneficent author of infinite woe" (358).

24 James' *The Sacred Fount* explicitly develops the theme of vampirism (whereby one person gains at another's expense) which Edel and others have identified as one of James' central themes. Vampirism seems particularly resonant in light of his own treatment and use of Minnie Templeton's life for his own art.

25 Those who are interested in "fixing" James's sexuality as homosexual might argue here that James, via Ralph, via Isabel, was seeking an intimacy with male partners. See Leland S. Person's "Henry James, George Sand, and the Suspense of Masculinity." Also see Eve Sedgwick's "The Beast in the Closet" in *Epistemology of the Closet* and William Veeder's "Henry James and the Uses of the Feminine." Veeder sees the male characters in *Portrait* as being as passive as the female, calling them "emasculate men inhabit[ing] the condition of the "feminine" (230). In *The Art of Criticism*, Veeder and Susan M. Griffin write that "Henry James himself combined the feminine and the masculine" (3).

For more on sexuality in James, see Kelly Cannon, *Henry James and Masculinity*; and Priscilla L. Walton, *The Disruption of the Feminine in Henry James*.

26 For a study of the overwhelming sense of powerlessness in *Portrait of a Lady* see William Veeder, "The Portrait of a Lack."

CHAPTER FIVE

1 Russo, *I.A. Richards: His Life and Work*, 406.

2 Hardy, *Tess of the d'Urbervilles* ed. Grindle and Gatrell, 128. All subsequent references in the text will refer to this edition.

3 See Silverman's "History, Figuration and Female Subjectivity in *Tess of the d'Urbervilles*," 23.

4 The title of Miller's book on Hardy is *Thomas Hardy: Distance and Desire*.

5 About a similar attempt at subjectification (Freud's account of a girl's coming of age), Teresa de Lauretis has written: "The myth of which she is presumed to be the subject ... in fact works to construct *her* as a 'personified obstacle' ... And so her story, like any other story, is a question of his desire" (*Alice Doesn't*, 133).

6 John Goode writes, "Tess is the subject of the novel: that makes her inevitably an object of the reader's consumption (no novel has ever produced so much of what Sontag required in place of hermeneutics, namely, an erotics of art)" ("Sue Bridehead and the New Woman," 102).

7 In James vision is more persistently connected to knowledge and power (see Bersani's "The Jamesian Lie" and "The Subject of Power" and Seltzer's *Henry James and the Art of Power*). In *The Scarlet Letter*, vision is linked to one emotion: shame.

8 There is of course nothing new in this type of seduction. The paintings that Diderot most admired, by Greuze for example, portrayed young women, none of whom actively seduced the gaze, but who appear, to the twentieth-century eye at least, very coy and sentimental. See Fried, *Absorption and Theatricality*.

9 See David Lodge, "Thomas Hardy and Cinematographic Form."

10 In *Distance and Desire* Miller writes, "At a distance in time and yet present as the events occur, a cold observer, spatially detached, seeing without being seen, and yet at the same time able to share the feelings of the characters, see with their eyes, and hear with their ears – a paradoxical combination of proximity and distance, presence and

absence, sympathy and coldness, characterizes the narrator whose role Hardy plays" (55).

11 This coaching of the reader to see and distinguish Tess, is, as I remarked earlier, similar to the encouragement we receive in James' *Portrait* to love and appreciate the heroine in spite of her "smallness" and seeming insignificance. In *Clarissa*, by contrast, the heroine is always already marked and distinguished by her virtue and her beauty. Similarly, Hester has been marked before the novel even opens.

12 This, of course, is Tess's accusation and lament when Angel arrives to find her at the boardinghouse with Alec (513), and it was also the original title of the novel, *Too Late, Beloved* (see Jacobus, "Tess's Purity," 321).

13 J.H. Miller, in *Fiction and Repetition*, writes, "Time in this novel is this failure of fit" (137).

14 There is a similar emphasis on the effects of distance and elevation of perspective in *The Portrait*. Isabel, in chapter 42, thinks, "Osmond's beautiful mind indeed seemed to peep down from a small high window and mock at her" (360). In *The Scarlet Letter* the narrator notes, "While Hester stood in that magic circle of ignominy ... the admirable preacher was looking down from the sacred pulpit" (167). In these two cases, as in *Tess*, the reader is encouraged to feel sympathy, concern, and even mild outrage at the heroines' lower positions.

15 In this sense, whether caught in the headlights of the train or in Angel's gaze, Tess comes to resemble the prisoner of Jeremy Bentham's panopticon who, as Foucault puts it in *Discipline and Punish*, "is seen, but ... does not see' (200). "Disciplinary power," he writes, "is exercised through its [own] invisibility [but] ... it imposes on those whom it subjects a principle of compulsory visibility" (187). See chapter 3 above.

16 Rooney, "'A Little More than Persuading'" 96. See also Carol Siegel who writes that "Tess is woman as a trope for victimization. Almost every contact she has with others inscribes her victimization. She takes victimhood beyond gender ... She even lends it to whatever man enters her life. But then she genders it feminine again, for if she is, as Hardy names her, a pure woman, her story defines pure womanhood, that is female essence, as victimization" (*Male Masochism*, 44–5).

17 See also Rooney's "Criticism and the Subject of Sexual Violence," for a fascinating discussion of the way that various critics have attempted to deal with the subject of Tess and Clarissa's rape/seductions (1269–78).

18 This would seem to be Tess's own assessment. On her trip to Flint-comb Ash, she purposefully hides her figure and face, even cutting off her eyebrows. See also this scene with Alec: "'Don't look at me like that!' he said abruptly. Tess, who had been quite unconscious of her action and mien, instantly withdrew the large dark gaze of her eyes ... And there was revived in her the wretched sentiment which had often come to her before, that, in inhabiting the fleshly tabernacle with which nature had endowed her she was somehow doing wrong" (425).

CHAPTER SIX

1 Angela Carter, *Nights at the Circus* 290.
2 Jan Garden Castro, "An Interview with Margaret Atwood," in Kathrynn VanSpanckeren and Jan Garden Castro, eds., *Margaret Atwood: Vision and Form*, 219. Atwood is referring here to the sentence in *Surfacing*: "This above all, to refuse to be a victim."
3 The phrase, "talking back," comes from bell hooks' book of the same name. She writes: "In the world of the southern black community I grew up in, 'back talk' and 'talking back' meant speaking as an equal to an authority figure. It meant daring to disagree and sometimes it just meant having an opinion ... [It] was a courageous act – an act of risk and daring" (5). It is this sense of risk, courage, and rebellion that I want to preserve.
4 I use Atwood and Carter here as representatives of a larger class of writers. I do not mean to imply that they are alone in this undertaking. There have been, and continue to be, legions of feminist writers working at this task.
5 Sedgwick writes: "Girard traced a calculus of power that was structured by the relation of rivalry between the two active members of an erotic triangle. What is most interesting for our purposes in his study is his insistence that, in any erotic rivalry, the bond that links the two rivals is as intense and potent as the the bond that links either of the rivals to the beloved" (*Between Men*, 21).
6 According to Rachel Brownstein, the heroine's desire is for action, and it is from this primary desire that female readers construct their own: "Novel heroines, like novel readers, are often women who want to become heroines." (*Becoming a Heroine*, xv). But my question is: what if men also want to become heroines?
7 The idea of the novel as the vehicle of desire is as old as the novel

form itself. *Don Quixote* and *Madame Bovary* are two of the most famous examples, novels which deal with the after-effects of novel sickness.

8 I am thinking here of such obvious examples as the verb "to master" meaning to learn, or the adjective "seminal," meaning original and productive.

9 Henrietta has her Mr Bantling, Anna Howe her Mr Hickman. The joke in their portrayal is that each will so undoubtedly lead her husband by the nose.

10 On gender roles in *The Scarlet Letter*, see T. Walter Herbert who calls Dimmesdale a "womanly man" and Hester "a manly woman." "Nathaniel Hawthorne, Una Hawthorne, and *The Scarlet Letter*" 285.

David Leverenz writes that Hester "realizes that her winning advice to Dimmesdale – 'Preach! Write! Act! Do anything, save to lie down and die' can apply only to men, not to herself." "Mrs. Hawthorne's Headache" 560.

11 See Henrietta Stackpole's exclamation to Isabel in *The Portrait*, "Oh, you do give me such a sense of helplessness!" (546). See also William Veeder, who writes that "At war in James are the life and death drives as Freud defined them." "The Feminine Orphan and the Emergent Master," 198.

12 What I am arguing against here is the tendency in feminist film scholarship to think of voyeurism as male and as sadistic.

This view, so pervasive for a while, has been challenged more frequently lately. For example, Carole-Anne Tyler writes, "As D.N. Rodowick has pointed out, Mulvey's almost biologizing insistence on aligning the cinematic gaze with masculinity and an active and controlling voyeurism and fetishism is masochistic rather than sadistic." "Boys Will be Girls," 46. See also, Regina Schwartz, "Rethinking Voyeurism and Patriarchy: The Case of Paradise Lost."

13 There is both pleasure and power in being the object of another's gaze. As Michael Ann Holly puts it, "The person who does the looking is the person with the power. No doubt about it; looking is power, but so too, is the ability to make someone look." "Past Looking," 395.

14 In his introduction to the *The Dialogic Imagination* Michael Holquist writes, "'Novel' is the name Bakhtin gives to whatever force is at work within a given literary system to reveal the limits, the artificial constraints of that system," xxxi.

15 "But then I realized it wasn't the men I hated, it was the Americans, the human beings men and women both." Atwood, *Surfacing*, 154.

16 They feel that they are living in "occupied territory" (121).

17 Frank Davey notes the centrality of the Gothic in Atwood's work. The Gothic, after all, is the literature of fear; it exploits the erotics of fear and helplessness. He writes: "There is so much Gothic imagery – of dismemberment, trick mirrors, dungeons, mazes, disembowellings – in [Atwood's work]." *Margaret Atwood*, 65.

18 Grace writes of "her need to keep diving in order to surface" (*Violent Duality*, 106).

19 In this scene Joe is portrayed as being in a similarly liminal state. He waits, "balancing on the dock which is neither land nor water" (192). The amphibious state would appear to be important to Atwood's vision of liminality. Frogs appear countless times, as laboratory specimens in jars, as bait on fishing hooks, as creatures of the place in which she learns to feel at home.

20 She acts as a rescuer when she empties all of the men's film into the lake, film that included degrading shots of Anna (166).

21 In *Surfacing*, the narrator muses, "I thought of how it would appear in the history books when it was over: a paragraph with dates and a short summary of what happened" (97).

Arnold Davidson writes, "As Atwood has noted to Cathy N. Davidson in an interview, this is 'what happens to history – something that's a very intense experience for the people who are living it becomes a subject of speculation, often of witticism, and rather detached analysis two hundred years later.'" "A Feminist 1984," *Ms.* February 17, 1986 24–6. Quoted in "Future Tense."

Another point of comparison is the similarity between the fate of Offred's tapes and Clarissa's papers. Clarissa's papers are edited by Belford, an assignment he takes on as an almost sacred trust in reverence for her memory. There is no such reverence apparent in Professor Pieixoto's attitude. The two situations are, nevertheless, more similar than they might first appear. In each case we read the woman's words after she has died, and in each case the effect is a heightening of pathos. We feel for her because of what she has undergone *and* because she never got to tell her story directly. The difficulty in its telling is as much a part of the story as the events themselves.

22 In *Tess* the narrator used a similar technique which I called cinematic. The narratorial point of view was first established as Tess's own and then radically altered to construct her at a distance as, for example, a

fly on the landscape (see chapter 5.) Atwood, I am arguing, is using the method, almost cynically, to heighten reader response.

23 Arnold Davidson writes that what is portrayed is "an appalling future already implicit in the contemporary world," and "in a very real sense, the future presaged by *The Handmaid's Tale* is already *our* history" "Future Tense," (113, 116).

24 It seems to me that *The Handmaid's Tale* owes more than its theme and setting to *The Scarlet Letter*. Both share the same sense of fear and paranoia, numbness and despair.

25 See Nicole Ward Jouve, "'Mother is a Figure of Speech …'" on Carter, mothers, Bataille, Kristeva, and Irigaray.

26 For more on the Bluebeard tale, its origins and some of its contemporary applications, see Sherrill E. Grace, "Courting Bluebeard."

27 Carter's concern here appears to be an investigation of a question similar to J. Benjamin's referred to above: "How does it come about that femininity appears inextricably linked to … masochism, or that women seek their desire in … another?" (quoted in chapter 1).

28 Several critics have made virtually the same point. Among them are Robert Clark, who asks, "In what ways do the novels of Angela Carter helps [sic] us to know patriarchy? In what ways do they reinscribe it?" ("Angela Carter's Desire Machine," 148). Patricia Duncker sees the problem as being one of form: "Carter is rewriting the tales within the strait-jacket of their original structures … so that shifting the perspective … merely explains, amplifies and re-produces rather than alters the original, deeply, rigidly sexist psychology of the erotic" ("Re-Imagining the Fairy Tales," 6). Avis Lewallen cites the title story as particularly disturbing: "Of all the tales in the volume I found 'The Bloody Chamber' most troubling in terms of female sexuality, largely because of the very seductive quality of the writing itself." She goes on to say that she felt "unease at being manipulated by the narrative to sympathise with masochism" ("Wayward Girls," 151). One critic who sees a radical potential in Carter's reworking of the fairy tales is Sylvia Bryant who claims that Carter is doing what Teresa de Lauretis urges in *Alice Doesn't*, that is subverting and rewriting the Oedipal pattern of narrative ("Re-Constructing Oedipus," 441).

29 Paulina Palmer, "From 'Coded Mannequin' to Bird Woman," 182.

30 Palmer writes that the images in the novel "represent ideas of liberation and rebirth; they evoke, in Cixous' words, 'the possibility of radical transformations.'" (Helene Cixous, *Sorties*, trans. Anne Liddle in

Elaine Marks and Isabelle de Courtivron (eds), *New French Feminisms*, 180. See also Rory P.B. Turner, "Subjects and Symbols."

31 In its sense of time it appears to work in a fashion diametrically opposed to that of *The Handmaid's Tale*. Atwood looks forward and sees the past. Carter looks backward and sees the future.

32 Lorna Sage writes that "Fevvers is a fictive mutant, 'a new kind of being'. Except that, of course, iconographically speaking, she's far from original. She's Leda *and* the swan, she's the Winged Victory of Samothrace, she's an angel, even. The image of the woman with wings has served throughout the centuries as a carrier of men's meanings, and at the turn of the century in particular this time-honoured icon had a new lease of life" *Angela Carter* 47.

CHAPTER SEVEN

1 Nancy K. Miller, *The Heroine's Text* 149.
2 For more on the way that novels have influenced women's lives, see Nancy Armstrong, *Desire and Domestic Fiction*.
3 I also pointed out the similarity between Rimbaud's statement and Flaubert's famous, "Madame Bovary, c'est moi."
4 I am thinking here particularly of a site such as James describes in his preface to *The Ambassadors*: "At the window of his wide, quite sufficiently wide, consciousness we are seated, from that admirable position we 'assist.'" (*Art of the Novel* 37).
5 In many ways the epistolary novel *is* the first novel. In its use of one letter contradicting and exposing the next, we see dialogism in its simplest and perhaps even most effective form.

Bibliography

Abrams, M.H. *The Mirror and the Lamp: Romantic Theory and the Critical Tradition*. New York: Oxford University Press, 1953.

Anesko, Michael. *"Friction with the Market": Henry James and the Profession of Authorship*. New York: Oxford University Press, 1986.

Armstrong, Nancy. *Desire and Domestic Fiction: A Political History of the Novel*. New York: Oxford University Press, 1987.

– ed., with Leonard Tennenhouse. *The Violence of Representation: Literature and the History of Violence*. London: Routledge, 1989.

Atwood, Margaret. *The Handmaid's Tale*. Toronto: Seal-McClelland-Bantam, 1989.

– "Running with the Tigers." Lorna Sage, *Flesh and the Mirror: Essays on the Art of Angela Carter* 117–35.

– *Surfacing*. Toronto: McClelland and Stewart, 1983.

Bakhtin, Mikhail. *The Dialogic Imagination*. Trans. Caryl Emerson and Michael Holquist. Ed. Michael Holquist. Austen: University of Texas Press, 1981.

– *Problems of Dostoevsky's Poetics*. Ed. and trans. Caryl Emerson. Theory and History of Literature, vol. 8. Minneapolis: University of Minnesota Press, 1984.

Bate, Walter Jackson. "The Sympathetic Imagination in Eighteenth-Century Criticism." *English Literary History* 12 (1945): 144–64.

Benjamin, Jessica. *The Bonds of Love: Psychoanalysis, Feminism, and the Problem of Domination*. New York: Pantheon Books, 1988.

-"A Desire of One's Own: Psychoanalytic Feminism and Intersubjective Space." Teresa de Lauretis, *Feminist Studies/Critical Studies*. 78–101.

Bercovitch, Sacvan. "The A-Politics of Ambiguity in *The Scarlet Letter*." *New Literary History* 19, no. 3 (1988):629–54.

– "Hawthorne's A-Morality of Compromise." *Representation* 24 (1988): 1-27.

Bersani, Leo. "The Jamesian Lie." *Partisan Review* 36 (1969):53–79.

– "Representation and Its Discontents." In *Allegory and Representation*, ed. Stephen J. Greenblatt, 145–62. Baltimore: Johns Hopkins University Press, 1981.

– "The Subject of Power." *diacritics* 7, no. 3 (1977):2–21.

Boumelha, Penny. *Thomas Hardy and Women: Sexual Ideology and Narrative Form*. Sussex: Harvester, 1982.

Brodhead, Richard H. "Sparing the Rod: Discipline and Fiction in Antebellum America." *Representations* 21 (1988):67–96.

Brownstein, Rachel M. *Becoming a Heroine: Reading about Women in Novels*. New York: Viking, 1982.

Butler, Judith. *Bodies that Matter: On the Discursive Limits of "Sex."* New York: Routledge, 1993.

– *Gender Trouble: Feminism and the Subversion of Identity*. New York: Routledge, 1990.

Bryant, Sylvia. "Re-Constructing Oedipus Through 'Beauty and the Beast.'" *Criticism*. 31, no. 4 (1989):439–53.

Cannon, Kelly. *Henry James and Masculinity: The Man at the Margins*. New York: St Martin's, 1993.

Carroll, David. *The Subject in Question: The Languages of Theory and The Strategies of Fiction*. Chicago: University of Chicago Press, 1982.

Carson, James. "Narrative Cross-Dressing and the Critique of Authorship in the Novels of Richardson." Goldsmith 95–113.

Carter, Angela. *The Bloody Chamber and Other Stories*. London: Victor Gollancz, 1979.

– *Nights at the Circus*. 1984. London: Pan, Picador, 1985.

Carton, Eva. "A Daughter of the Puritans and Her Old Master: Hawthorne, Una, and the Sexuality of Romance." In *Daughters and Fathers*. ed. Lynda E. Boose, and Betty S. Flowers, 208–32. Baltimore: Johns Hopkins University Press, 1989.

Castle, Terry. *Clarissa's Ciphers: Meaning and Disruption in Richardson's Clarissa*. Ithaca: Cornell University Press, 1982.

Castro, Jan Garden. "An Interview with Margaret Atwood." In *Margaret Atwood: Vision and Form*. VanSpanckeren and Castro 215–32.

Chai, Leon. *The Romantic Foundations of the American Renaissance.* Ithaca: Cornell University Press, 1978.

Clark, Robert. "Angela Carter's Desire Machine." *Women's Studies* 14 (1987):147–61.

Cohn, Dorrit. *Transparent Minds: Narrative Modes for Presenting Consciousness in Fiction.* Princeton: Princeton University Press, 1978.

Culler, Jonathan. *On Deconstruction: Theory and Criticism After Structuralism.* Ithaca: Cornell University Press, 1982.

Davey, Frank. *Margaret Atwood: A Feminist Poetics.* Vancouver: Talon-Books, 1984.

Davidson, Arnold. "Future Tense: Making History in *The Handmaid's Tale.*" VanSpanckeren and Castro 113–21.

Davis, Lennard J. *Factual Fictions: The Origins of the English Novel.* New York: Columbia University Press, 1983.

De Lauretis, Teresa. *Alice Doesn't: Feminism, Semiotics, Cinema.* Bloomington: Indiana University Press, 1984.

– ed. *Feminist Studies/Critical Studies.* Theories of Contemporary Culture 8. Bloomington: Indiana University Press, 1986.

– *Technologies of Gender: Essays on Theory, Film and Fiction.* Theories of Representation and Difference. Bloomington: Indiana University Press, 1987.

– "The Violence of Rhetoric." In *The Violence of Representation: Literature and the History of Violence.* ed. Nancy Armstrong, and Leonard Tennenhouse, 239-258. London: Routledge, 1989.

Diderot, Denis. "Éloge de Richardson." (1761) *Eighteenth Century French Novelists and the Novel.* Ed. and trans. Lawrence W. Lynch. York, SC: French Literary Publications Co., 1979. 121-35.

Doane, Mary Anne. *The Desire to Desire: The Woman's Film of the 1940s.* Bloomington: Indiana University Press, 1987.

– "Film and Masquerade: Theorizing the Female Spectator." *Screen* 23, nos. 3–4 (1982):74–87.

– Patricia Mellencamp, and Linda Williams, eds. *Re-Vision: Essays in Feminist Film Criticism.* Frederick, MD: University Publications of America, 1984.

Dryden, Edgar A. *Nathaniel Hawthorne: The Poetics of Enchantment.* Ithaca: Cornell University Press, 1977.

Duncker, Patricia. "Re-Imagining the Fairy Tales: Angela Carter's Bloody Chambers." *Literature and History* 10, no. 1 (1984):3–14.

Eagleton, Terry. *The Rape of Clarissa: Writing, Sexuality and Class Struggle in Samuel Richardson.* Oxford: Basil Blackwell, 1982.

Edel, Leon. Introduction. *The Portrait of a Lady*. By Henry James. Riverside Edition. Boston: Houghton Mifflin, 1963. v–xx.

Erens, Patricia, ed. *Issues in Feminist Film Criticism*. Bloomington: Indiana University Press, 1990.

Felman, Shoshana. *What Does a Woman Want: Reading and Sexual Difference*. Baltimore: Johns Hopkins University Press, 1993

– "Woman and Madness: The Critical Phallacy." *diacritics* 5, no. 4
(1975):2–10.

Fetterley, Judith. *The Resisting Reader: A Feminist Approach to American
Fiction*. Bloomington: Indiana University Press, 1978.

Flynn, Elizabeth A., and Patrocinio P. Schweickart, eds. *Gender and Reading: Essays on Readers, Texts, and Contexts*. Baltimore: Johns Hopkins
University Press, 1986.

Foucault, Michel. *Discipline and Punish: The Birth of the Prison*. Trans.
Alan Sheridan. New York: Random House, 1977.

– *The Foucault Reader*. Ed. Paul Rabinow. New York: Pantheon, 1984.

– *Power/Knowledge: Selected Interviews and Other Writings 1972–1977*.
Ed. Colin Gordon. Trans. Colin Gordon, Leo Marshall, John Mepham,
and Kate Soper. Brighton, Sussex: The Harvester Press, 1980.

Fried, Michael. *Absorption and Theatricality: Painting and Beholder in the
Age of Diderot*. Berkeley: University of California Press, 1980.

Fuss, Diana. *Essentially Speaking: Feminism, Nature and Difference*. New
York: Routledge, 1989.

– *Identification Papers*. New York: Routledge, 1995.

– ed. *Inside/Out: Lesbian Theories, Gay Theories*. New York: Routledge,
1991.

Gallagher, Catherine. "George Eliot and *Daniel Deronda*: The Prostitute
and the Jewish Question." In *Sex, Politics and Science in the Nineteenth-
Century Novel*, ed. Ruth Bernard Yeazell, 39–62. Baltimore: Johns Hopkins University Press, 1986.

Gardiner, Judith Kegan. *Rhys, Stead, Lessing, and the Politics of Empathy*.
Bloomington: Indiana University Press, 1989.

Gilbert, Sandra M., and Susan Gubar, *The Madwoman in the Attic: The
Woman Writer and the Nineteenth-Century Literary Imagination* New
Haven: Yale University Press, 1979.

Gilmore, Michael. "The Commodity World of *The Portrait of a Lady*."
New England Quarterly 59, no. 1 (1986):51–74.

Giordano, Frank R. Jr. *"I'd Have My Life Unbe": Thomas Hardy's Self-
Destructive Characters*. University: University of Alabama Press, 1984.

Girard, Rene. *Deceit, Desire and the Novel: Self and Other in Literary*

Structure. Trans. Yvonne Freccero. Baltimore: Johns Hopkins University Press, 1961.

Goldsmith, Elizabeth C., ed. *Writing the Female Voice: Essays on Epistolary Literature*. Boston: Northeastern University Press, 1989.

Goode, John. "Sue Bridehead and the New Woman." In *Women Writing and Writing About Women*, ed. Mary Jacobus, 100–13. London: Croom Helm, 1979.

– *Thomas Hardy: The Offensive Truth*. Rereading Literature. Oxford: Basil Blackwell, 1988.

Grace, Sherrill E. "Courting Bluebeard with Bartok, Atwood, and Fowles: Modern Treatment of the Bluebeard Theme." *Journal of Modern Literature* 11, no. 2 (1984):245–62.

– *Violent Duality: A Study of Margaret Atwood*. Montreal: Véhicule, 1980.

Greenblatt, Stephen J. *Renaissance Self-Fashioning: From More to Shakespeare*. Chicago: University of Chicago Press, 1980.

Gwilliam, Tassie. *Samuel Richardson's Fictions of Gender*. Stanford: Stanford University Press, 1993.

Habegger, Alfred. *Henry James and the "Woman Business"*. Cambridge: Cambridge University Press, 1989.

Hardy, Evelyn. "The Self-Destructive Element in Tess's Character." *Thomas Hardy, A Critical Biography*. Rpt. in *Tess of the d'Urbervilles*. Norton Critical Edition, ed. Scott Elledge. New York: Norton & Co., 1965. 447–50.

Hardy, Thomas. *Tess of the d'Urbervilles*. 1891. Ed. Juliet Grindle and Simon Gatrell. Oxford: Clarendon, 1983.

Hawthorne, Nathaniel. *The Blithedale Romance*. 1852. New York: Penguin, 1983.

– *The Scarlet Letter*. 1850. New York: Norton, 1988.

Herbert, T. Walter. "Nathaniel Hawthorne, Una Hawthorne, and *The Scarlet Letter*: Interactive Selfhoods and the Cultural Construction of Gender." *PMLA* 103, no. 3 (1988):285–97.

Holly, Michael Ann. "Past Looking." *Critical Inquiry* 16, no. 2 (1990):371–96.

hooks, bell [Gloria Watkins]. *Talking Back: Thinking Feminist, Thinking Black*. Toronto: Between the Lines, 1988.

Hudson, Nicholas. "Arts of Seduction and the Rhetoric of *Clarissa*." *Modern Language Quarterly* 50, no. 1 (1990):25–43.

Hunt, Lester H. "*The Scarlet Letter*: Hawthorne's Theory of Moral Sentiments." *Philosophy and Literature* 8, no. 1 (1984):75–88.

Hutner, Gordon. *Secrets and Sympathy: Forms of Disclosure in Hawthorne's Novels*. Athens: University of Georgia Press, 1988.

Irigaray, Luce. *This Sex which Is Not One*. Trans. Catherine Porter with Carolyn Burke. Ithaca: Cornell University Press, 1985.

Iser, Wolfgang. *The Implied Reader: Patterns of Communication in Prose Fiction from Bunyan to Beckett*. Baltimore: Johns Hopkins University Press, 1974.

Jacobus, Mary. "Tess's Purity." *Essays in Criticism* 26 (1976):318–38.

– ed. *Reading Woman: Essays in Feminist Criticism*. Gender and Culture 7. New York: Columbia University Press, 1986.

– ed. *Women Writing and Writing about Women*. London: Croom Helm, 1979.

James, Henry. *The Art of the Novel*. London: Scribner's, 1934.

– *Letters*, vols 1 and 2. Ed. Leon Edel. Cambridge: Belknap Press of Harvard, 1974.

– *The Portrait of a Lady*. 1881. New York: NAL, 1963.

Jay, Martin. *Downcast Eyes: The Denigration of Vision in Twentieth-Century French Thought*. Berkeley: University of California Press, 1993.

Jouve, Nicole Ward. "'Mother Is a Figure of Speech ...'" In *Flesh and the Mirror: Essays on the Art of Angela Carter*, ed. Lorna Sage, 136–70. London: Virago, 1994.

Kahn, Madeleine. *Narrative Transvestism: Rhetoric and Gender in the Eighteenth-Century Novel*. Ithaca: Cornell University Press, 1991.

Kauffman, Linda. "Special Delivery: Twenty-First Century Epistolarity in *The Handmaid's Tale*." Goldsmith 221-244.

Lacan, Jacques. *Ecrits: A Selection*. Trans. Alan Sheridan. New York: Norton, 1977.

Laplanche, J., and J.-B. Pontalis. *The Language of Psychoanalysis*. Trans. Donald Nicholson-Smith. New York: Norton, 1973.

Leverenz, David. "Mrs Hawthorne's Headache: Reading *The Scarlet Letter*." *Nineteenth-Century Fiction* 37, no. 4 (1983):552–75.

Levine, Laura. "Men in Women's Clothing: Anti-theatricality and Effeminization from 1579 to 1642." *Criticism* 28, no. 2 (1986):121–43.

Lewallen, Avis. "Wayward Girls but Wicked Women?: Female Sexuality in Angela Carter's The Bloody Chamber." In *Perspectives in Pornography: Sexuality in Film and Literature*, ed. Gary Day and Clive Bloom, 144-158. London: Macmillan, 1988.

Lodge, David. "Thomas Hardy and Cinematographic Form." *Novel* 7, no. 3 (1974):246-54.

Lubbock, Percy. *The Craft of Fiction*. New York: Viking, 1957.

Male, Roy R. "Hawthorne and the Concept of Sympathy." *Proceedings of the Modern Language Association* 68 (1953):138–49.

Marshall, David. *The Figure of Theater: Shaftesbury, Defoe, Adam Smith and George Eliot.* New York: Columbia University Press, 1986.

– *The Surprising Effects of Sympathy.* Chicago: University of Chicago Press, 1988.

McMaster, Juliet. "The Portrait of Isabel Archer." *American Literature* 45 (1973):50–66.

Michael, John. "History and Romance, Sympathy amd Uncertainty: The Moral of Stones in Hawthorne's Marble Faun." *Proceedings of the Modern Language Association* 103 (1988):150–61.

Miller, J. Hillis. *Fiction and Repetition: Seven English Novels.* Cambridge: Harvard University Press, 1983.

– *Thomas Hardy: Distance and Desire.* Cambridge: Belknap-Harvard University Press, 1970.

Miller, Nancy K. *The Heroine's Text: Readings in the French and English Novel.* New York: Columbia University Press, 1980.

Mills, Sara. *Gendering the Reader.* New York: Harvester, 1994.

Moi, Toril. *Sexual/Textual Politics: Feminist Literary Theory.* London: Routledge, 1985.

Morgan, Thais E., ed. *Men Writing the Feminine: Literature, Theory and the Question of Genders.* Albany: State University of New York Press, 1994.

Morris, Pam. *Literature and Feminism: An Introduction.* Oxford: Blackwell, 1993.

Mulvey, Laura. *Visual and Other Pleasures.* Bloomington: Indiana University Press, 1989.

Niemtzow, Annette. "Marriage and the New Woman in *The Portrait of a Lady.*" *American Literature* 47, no. (1975):377–95.

Olsen, Tillie. *Silences.* New York: Delta, 1978.

Palmer, Paulina. "From 'Coded Mannequin' to Bird Woman: Angela Carter's Magic Flight." In *Women Reading Women's Writing,* ed. Sue Roe. 179-205. Sussex: Harvester, 1987.

Person, Leland S. "Henry James, George Sand, and the Suspense of Masculinity." *Proceedings of the Modern Language Association* 106, no. 3 (1991):515–28.

Poirier, Richard. *The Comic Sense of Henry James: A Study of the Early Novels.* London: Chatto and Windus, 1960.

Poulet, Georges. "Phenomenology of Reading." *New Literary History* 1, no. 1 (1969): 53–68.

Pratt, Annis. "*Surfacing* and the Rebirth Journey." In *The Art of Margaret Atwood: Essays in Criticism*, ed. Arnold E. Davidson and Cathy N. Davidson. 139–57. Toronto: Anansi, 1981.

Preston, John. *The Created Self: The Reader's Role in Eighteenth Century Fiction*. London: Heinemann, 1970.

Pritchett, V.S. *The Living Novel*. New York: Reynal and Hitchcock, 1947.

Richardson, Samuel. *Clarissa or, The History of a Young Lady*, 4 vols. 1747. New York: Everyman's Library, 1932.

Rodgers, James. "Sensibility, Sympathy, Benevolence: Physiology and Moral Philosophy in *Tristram Shandy*." In *Languages of Nature: Critical Essays on Science and Literature*, ed. L.J. Jordanova. London: Free Association Books, 1986.

Rooney, Ellen. "Criticism and the Subject of Sexual Violence." *Modern Language Notes* 98, no. 5 (1983):1269–278.

– "'A Little More than Persuading': Tess and the Subject of Sexual Violence." In *Rape and Representation*, ed. Lynn A. Higgins and Brenda R. Silver, 87–113. New York: Columbia University Press, 1991.

Rousseau, Jean-Jacques. *Letter to M. D'Alembert on the Theatre*. Trans. Allan Bloom. Glencoe, IL: The Free Press, 1960.

Russo, John Paul. *I.A. Richards: His Life and Work*. Baltimore: Johns Hopkins University Press. 1989.

Russo, Mary. "Female Grotesques: Carnival and Theory." In Teresa de Lauretis, *Feminist Studies/Critical Studies*. 213–29.

Sage, Lorna, *Angela Carter*, Plymouth: Nothcote House in association with the British Council, 1994

– ed. *Flesh and the Mirror: Essays on the Art of Angela Carter*. London: Virago Press, 1994.

Schor, Naomi. "French Feminism is a Universalism." *differences* 7, no. 1(1995):15–47.

Schwab, Gabriele. "Seduced by Witches: Nathaniel Hawthorne's *The Scarlet Letter* in the Context of New England Witchcraft Fictions." In *Seduction and Theory: Readings of Gender, Representation and Rhetoric*, ed. Dianne Hunter, 170–91. Urbana & Chicago: University of Illinois Press, 1989.

Schwartz, Regina. "Rethinking Voyeurism and Patriarchy: The Case of Paradise Lost." *Representations* 34, no. (1991):85–103.

Schweikart, Patrocinio P. "Reading Ourselves: Toward a Feminist Theory of Reading." In *Gender and Reading: Essays on Readers, Texts, and Contexts*, ed. Elizabeth A. Flynn and Patrocinio Schweikart, 31–62. Baltimore: Johns Hopkins University Press, 1986.

Sedgwick, Eve Kosofsky. *Between Men: English Literature and Male Homosocial Desire*. New York: Columbia University Press, 1985.

– *Epistemology of the Closet*. Berkeley: University of California Press, 1990.

Seltzer, Mark. *Henry James and the Art of Power*. Ithaca: Cornell University Press, 1984.

Showalter, Elaine. *A Literature of Their Own: British Women Novelists from Bronte to Lessing*. Princeton, NJ: Princeton University Press, 1977.

Siegel, Carol. *Male Masochism: Modern Revisions of the Story of Love*. Bloomington: Indiana University Press, 1995.

Silverman, Kaja. "History and Female Subjectivity in *Tess of the d'Urbervilles*." *Novel* 19, no. 2 (1984):5–28.

Smith, Adam. *The Theory of Moral Sentiments*. Oxford: Clarendon, 1976.

Stout, Janis B. "The Fallen Woman and the Conflicted Author: Hawthorne and Hardy." *American Transcendental Quarterly*. ns 1, no. 3 (1987):233–46.

Turner, Rory P.B. "Subjects and Symbols: Transformations of Identity in *Nights at the Circus*." *Folklore Forum* 20, nos. 1–2 (1987):39–60.

Turner, Victor. *The Ritual Process: Structure and Anti-Structure*. Chicago: University of Chicago Press, 1969.

Tyler, Carole-Anne. "Boys Will be Girls: The Politics of Gay Drag." In Diana Fuss, *Inside/Out: Lesbian Theories, Gay Theories*, 32–70.

VanSpanckeren, Kathryn, and Jan Garden Castro. *Margaret Atwood: Vision and Form*. Ad Feminam: Women and Literature 4. Carbondale: Southern Illinois University Press, 1988.

Veeder, William. "The Feminine Orphan and the Emergent Master" *Isabel Archer*. Ed. Harold Bloom. New York: Chelsea House, 1992.

– "Henry James and the Uses of the Feminine." In *Out of Bounds: Male Writers and Gender(ed) Criticism*, ed. Laura Claridge and Elizabeth Langland, 219–51. Amherst: University of Massachusetts Press, 1990.

– "The Portrait of a Lack." *New Essays on "The Portrait of a Lady."* Ed. Joel Porte. Cambridge: Cambridge University Press, 1990. 95–121.

– and Susan M. Griffin, eds. *The Art of Criticism: Henry James on the Theory and the Practice of Fiction*. Chicago: University of Chicago Press, 1986.

Vernon, John. *Money and Fiction: Literary Realism in the Nineteenth and Early Twentieth Centuries*. Ithaca: Cornell University Press, 1984.

Walton, Priscilla L. *The Disruption of the Feminine in Henry James*. Toronto: University of Toronto Press, 1992.

Warner, William Beatty. *Reading* Clarissa: *The Struggles of Interpretation.* New Haven: Yale University Press, 1979.

Watt, Ian. *The Rise of the Novel: Studies in Defoe, Richardson, and Fielding.* Berkeley: University of California Press, 1967.

White, Patricia. "Female Spectator, Lesbian Specter: *The Haunting.*" In Diana Fuss, *Inside/Out*, 142–72.

Yeazell, Ruth Bernard, ed. *Sex, Politics and Science in the Nineteenth-Century Novel.* Baltimore: Johns Hopkins University Press, 1986.

Index